THE DAILY MALE 2

THE DAILY MALE 2

The Lunchtime Edition

Nick Battle

Authentic

Copyright © 2010 Nick Battle

16 15 14 13 12 11 10   7 6 5 4 3 2 1

First published 2010 by Authentic Media Limited
Milton Keynes
www.authenticmedia.co.uk

The right of Nick Battle to be identified as the
Author of this work has been asserted by him in accordance with the
Copyright, Designs and Patents Act 1988

All rights reserved. No part of this publication may be reproduced, stored in
a retrieval system, or transmitted in any form or by any means, electronic,
mechanical, photocopying, recording or otherwise, without the prior
permission of the publisher or a licence permitting restricted copying. In the
UK such licences are issued by the Copyright Licensing Agency,
90 Tottenham Court Road, London, W1P 9HE

British Library Cataloguing in Publication Data

A catalogue record for this book is available from the British Library

ISBN: 978-1-86024-767-5

Scripture quotations marked NLT are taken from the Holy Bible, New Living
Translation, copyright © 1996, 2004. Used by permission of Tyndale House
Publishers, Inc., Wheaton, Illinois 60189. All rights reserved.

Cover Design by Norman Trotter
Cover photo by Tony Swain
Printed in Great Britain by J.F. Print, Sparkford

For my children
Misha, Jodie and Jesse
with love from Dad

Contents

Thanks / ix

Acknowledgements / xi

1. Accidents Will Happen / 1
2. Cash Cow / 4
3. Do You Know Where You're Going To? / 7
4. Fatboy Thin? / 10
5. Irreconcilable Differences? / 13
6. Oranges / 16
7. Step To It? / 19
8. Suffer the Children / 22
9. The Boyfriend / 25
10. Grace / 28
11. Breasts / 31
12. A Pint, a Pub and a Prayer / 34
13. Horses / 40
14. Cradle to the Grave / 42
15. Golden Slumbers / 45
16. Motorbikin' / 48
17. Prayer Power / 50
18. Spin or Sin? / 53
19. In God's Name? / 56
20. Hearts and Bones / 58
21. Stop the Traffik / 60
22. The Funny Bone / 63

23. The Critic / 66
24. Mothers / 68
25. Birthdays / 71
26. The Ascent of Man / 74
27. Hope / 77
28. Only the Good Die Young / 79
29. Treasures of Darkness / 81
30. Hair / 83
31. The Buggy Incident / 86
32. Job Titles / 89
33. What's Going On? / 92
34. Giving / 95
35. The Little Boy and the Sparrow / 97
36. Christmas / 100
37. Dentists / 102
38. The Sacred Loan / 105
39. The Labourer / 108
40. The Sweet Smell of Success / 111

The Gravel Road Trust / 114

Thanks

As an author this is one of my favourite parts of any book I've written and arguably the bit you will want to skip. For me, however, it's where I get to say thank you to the people who made it possible for you to hold this slim tome in your hands. I'm aware of just how much faith and trust Authentic Media have invested in me in the last couple of years, for which I'd like to say a very big thank you.

Especially to the following people: Liz Williams for all her sterling work in making sure everything comes together once I've finally handed in the finished manuscript; Gareth Russell for his drive and vision and how he gets the job done; and especially my publisher Malcolm Down who got me started in the first place.

Finally, thanks to my wife Nicky and our children Misha, Jodie and Jesse. What a blessing it is to know and love you all.

As always, to God be the glory.

February 2009
Chorleywood, England

Acknowledgements

I would like to thank:

Ruth Dearnley, CEO of Stop The Traffik, for her opinion and feedback on the eponymous chapter.

David and Carrie Grant, for twenty years of wonderful friendship. Many miles travelled, many more to go!

Clive Price, for once again riding shotgun and editing my rants and raves.

Ian Slade, Alan Richards, J.John and The Philo Trust, for their unwavering support, and also the Gravel Road Trust, particularly Tim Bradford, Alun Price-Davies, John Macaulay, Yvonne Cooke, James Roberts, Graham Cleveland, Jon Cobb and Nick Corden.

St Andrew's Church and the wonderful people who have supported us as family these past fifteen years.

Finally, thank you to those of you who have bought my previous books and written letters and/or emails of encouragement. It is always wonderful to hear from you.

1

ACCIDENTS WILL HAPPEN

'There should be no poor among you.'
(Deuteronomy 15:4)

What is it about the weather? I've often wished I'd been born in sunnier climes – as opposed to bracing old Blighty, with its rainy days and overcast skies that remind me of a gun-metal-grey Lowry landscape. Isn't it bizarre that what happens to us, just by a simple accident of birth, can make us or break us?

> If God is in control, **why is there so much ugly stuff in the world?**

I wasn't born in a slum into poverty on the outskirts of Kampala in Uganda. I wasn't born to a single mother who'd been raped by an uncle and brought into a neighbourhood full of disease, disaster and death. I was born at a country hospital in picturesque Devon. My parents were married. I benefited from education, clothing and shelter that I took to be my birthright.

Indeed, I understood it to be normal that, as a child, I should have these things.

I was brought up to believe in God, Manchester United and my mate Marmite. I never knew the fear of hunger or the threat of *real* violence. Even when we lived in the north of England, I was always warm. The most menacing illness I encountered in my youth was chickenpox. Oh yes, and maybe mumps.

So just what kind of twisted lottery are we involved in? And where is God when the wheel of fortune spins? Why are some of us awarded comfortable lives and others, by comparison, are given grinding poverty and pain? Is it just a case of 'Accidents will happen'?

I don't think so.

If God is in control, why is there so much ugly stuff in the world? Oh, I know we can argue it's as a result of sin, avarice, selfishness and greed. But I'm afraid that explanation isn't enough. I don't want textbook answers and qualified theological reasoning any more.

> Maybe I've been living in the **kingdom of comfort** for too long

I want the truth. Plain and simple. I have to know.

And I may be a 50-something middle-class milksop pouring his heart out as he types on his Powerbook G4 – the price of which could educate and feed four children for a year in certain parts of the globe – but you know, it just doesn't feel right. Maybe I've been living in the kingdom of comfort for too long. Maybe my whole life has given me an emotional immune system that has become so adept at not seeing the real issues, that when they come along I bat them away like an annoying fly.

Maybe it's time I changed.

God, I know you're listening. Help me. Answer my prayer.

> **NICK'S NOTES**
>
> ✔ GIVE AS MUCH AS YOU CAN AFFORD (BE HONEST HERE) TO A RELIEF AGENCY WORKING AMONG THE POOREST COMMUNITIES ON EARTH.
>
> ✔ KEEP IN TOUCH WITH ALL THE LATEST NEWS FROM DEVELOPING NATIONS BY BECOMING A REGULAR SUPPORTER OF A CHARITY WORKING IN THOSE REGIONS.
>
> ✔ ALWAYS, ALWAYS, THINK OF OTHERS LESS FORTUNATE THAN YOU.

2

CASH COW

'Wisdom and money can get you almost anything, but only wisdom can save your life.'
(Ecclesiastes 7:12)

It's that time of year again. If I listen very carefully, I can hear Sir Cliff in the distance singing 'Summer Holiday' and the sound of the Atlantic Ocean, waves breaking, calling me down to Cornwall. But what does it mean for a large percentage of the population?

> When things are going well – save

Forced to dig deeper into pockets that seem to be emptying at an alarming rate, most of us have been hit with property prices spiralling down. A lot of people are facing redundancy and we're now officially *in recession*. So just where do we go for our holidays? Not surprisingly, most of us Brits are choosing to stay at home. Aside from the moral implications of our carbon footprint, it is, hopefully, cheaper – even if the weather is determined to remain staunchly unpredictable.

But even filling up the family Toyota Picnic (the height of motoring luxury☺) now costs close to £60 – when it used to be £45. Cutbacks seem to be all the rage. And for anyone who is self-employed, as I am, companies are simply no longer outsourcing (business babble for giving work to people who are outside the organization).

For a while it's possible to shore up the family finances by flogging old CDs on Amazon and eBay. But once you've exhausted your precious supply of musical memories, where do you go next? No – not the vinyl! Stay away from my David Bowie records!

Surely not? Is nothing sacred?

The simple answer is, *no*. While I have a major rethink about starting a new career as I approach my fifty-first birthday, I will do whatever it takes (as long as it's legal) to keep the good ship *Battle* afloat.

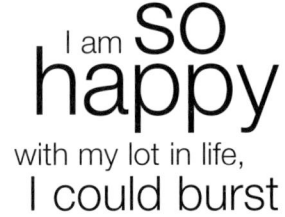

Once upon a time I was a veritable 'cash cow' with money on tap 24/7. The silly thing is, when things are going well, we tend to presume life will always carry on this way. If only it did!

Here's a tip. When things are going well – *save*. Yes, give money away and *always* tithe. But save. Chances are there will always be a rainy day, and that's not Nick being pessimistic. It's just the way life is sometimes. Actually, often. You know – the car makes a funny noise, the boiler starts leaking and the washing machine no longer washes whiter than white.

Nearly always at the same time. So be ready.

On the plus side, I am so happy with my lot in life, I could burst. However, I am choosing not to do this, as I believe it could have a profound and long-lasting effect on the environment.

Cash cows and golden calves. They're all just silly moos.

> **NICK'S NOTES**
>
> ✔ BE CAREFUL WITH YOUR MONEY, BUT BE GENEROUS TOO.
>
> ✔ EVEN IF YOU FEEL REDUNDANT, YOU'RE NOT. GOD HAS GOT A PLAN FOR YOU.

3

DO YOU KNOW WHERE YOU'RE GOING TO?

'Make your way plain for me to follow.'
(Psalm 5:8)

It's a question I keep asking myself more and more at the moment. I know my eternal destination. And I thank God for that. But from time to time, on a day-to-day basis, I get a little confused. You see, I'm in the middle of the 'male menopause', for want of a better term. 'What,' I hear you cry, 'has he lost the plot completely? I thought only women went through that!'

Allow me to explain.

It's that time of life when the children are starting perhaps to leave the nest – and hopefully the

Nobody on this earth has **all the answers**

mortgage isn't quite as crippling as it used to be. It's that time of life when the more affluently afflicted male is thinking about tinkering with a sports car – and the less financially blessed of us are rummaging about in our potting sheds searching for a little bit of peace and quiet.

Perhaps you face the mirror, vainly trying to suck in your stomach. Perhaps you are struggling to reposition your few strands of hair to emulate your boyhood hero, Man United's legendary centre forward Bobby Charlton. You still look at and admire women in their twenties and thirties. But you know they'll never find you attractive. That is, not unless you're filthy stinking rich and/or dead famous. Then the shallow ones will flicker round like moths to a flame. In the process, you may well get extinguished and their ardour may well fade.

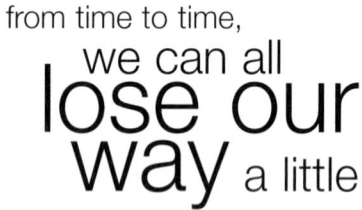

from time to time, we can all lose our way a little

You're not ready to accept the inevitable. Yet you no longer sit behind the wheel of the car doing 120 mph just for the fun of it. Life is beginning to move to a different rhythm and purpose. If you're still married – well done to both of you! If you find yourself alone, please know you are not.

You see, sometimes life is like a T-shirt that says, 'Don't follow me, I'm lost too'. Nobody on this earth has all the answers. Do I know where I'm going to? Well, not today. No, I don't. I'm a bit confused. I know I'm a husband and a father. I can write a bit. I can play the odd instrument or two. I've even been known to proclaim the glories of the kingdom (given the right climatic conditions and a prevailing wind). But from time to time, we can all lose our way a little.

I'm reminded of that awful American bumper-sticker which says, 'God is my co-pilot'. Perhaps on days like this, that slogan isn't really enough. Maybe on days like this, we should simply say, 'Jesus, take the wheel.'

I, for one, have taken too many wrong turns not to let him drive.

> **NICK'S NOTES**
>
> ✔ LOCK THE DOOR ON THAT POTTING SHED AND GET OUT MORE.
> ✔ SPEND MORE TIME WITH YOUR CLOSEST MATES, SHARE YOUR DREAMS AND LAUGH A LOT.
> ✔ ASK GOD, 'WHAT DO YOU WANT ME TO DO?' THIS QUESTION ISN'T FOR WIMPS!

4

FATBOY THIN?

'The dagger went so deep that the handle disappeared beneath the king's fat.'
(Judges 3:22)

'Let me have men about me that are fat!' said Julius Caesar. Or something like that. He was a man of considerable discernment. In Uganda – and probably in some Texan barbecue joints – I am considered extraordinarily attractive because of my girth. Yes, I am fat. I have got to this part-time somnambulistic state through a process of – let's be frank here – over-indulgence.

Yes, I am fat

But I'm a product of the pop industry. Back in the days when I didn't know where my next meal was coming from, whenever I did get fed, I would fall on my food like a rabid hyena who'd just discovered a fresh ibis corpse deep in the Transvaal. When I finally discovered employment and a living wage – not to mention that magic wishing-well most people call *expenses* – I didn't look back.

I stuffed myself.

At the time of writing, I weigh 220 pounds in my socks, and am just 5 feet 8 inches tall. My doctor told me I was on the cusp of being 'clinically obese'. I felt like saying, 'You're on the cusp of being flattened.' Somehow I managed to restrain myself. You see, it's nobody's fault but mine. And now I have to set about some kind of exercise regime to get rid of all this corpulence. And we all know, don't we, how flippin' hard that is.

So, 'Once more into the breach, dear friends' (or something like that). Out I go into the hot noonday sun or cold winter snow, pushing my baby son in his pram (sorry – I should say, 'baby travelling system'!), with my faithful mutt Max at my side, for an hour of reluctant exercise.

What's the alternative? Liposuction? Even if I could afford it, have you seen what they do – pummelling away with what looks like a giant knitting-needle-cum-hoover? It's probably less painful to get whacked by the Welsh Dragon, Joe Calzaghe. Have you *seen* the elastic band they put round your stomach? Apparently the ladies advocate it. Fern Britton and Sharon Osborne have had astonishing results.

Nah! None of that feels natural to me. The bottom line is (yes, pun intended) – I need to eat and drink less, and exercise more.

Now, where's my leotard and leggings?

NICK'S NOTES

✔ DIETS ARE A SHORT-TERM SOLUTION.

✔ LOOK AT YOUR LIFESTYLE.

✔ BUILD IN REGULAR EXERCISE.

5

IRRECONCILABLE DIFFERENCES?

'Forgive anyone who offends you.'
(Colossians 3:13)

What can we do when we see two dear friends at odds with each other? Sometimes people we've known for a long time – like married couples or best mates – inexplicably suddenly seem to implode. Harsh words, wild rumours and cruel accusations start to fly. Bitterness and sub-texts creep into every conversation. In the end, you don't know who to believe.

I've witnessed this among two of my dearest friends. At the risk of sounding melodramatic, it breaks my heart. And the devil loves a good wind-up, to get in the middle of things, creating even more havoc, playing on insecurities, latent fears and innuendo.

Sadly, the more we talk about it, the worse it gets. Careless talk costs relationships and adds fuel to the fire.

An untreated wound can become **poisonous**

People in positions of leadership are no exception – as anybody who watched Tony Blair's slow, tortuous exit from Number 10, Downing Street, will attest. It was an undignified way to go, clinging on to wring every last drop out of the premiership while your former best friend and ally – to whom you promised the job – is standing on the touchline with steam coming out of his ears. It can be the same in churches. Sometimes when a leader is appointed, it has taken so long that momentum gets lost, people lose heart and some may leave.

An untreated wound can become poisonous. The infection can spread. Ultimately it may kill. I believe it's the same with unforgiveness. If we cannot reconcile our differences, it eats at us, gnawing away like a dog chewing a bone. But the bone keeps being buried, dug up, chewed, then buried again.

> Clear the air and try to do it in a **loving** manner

Sharp words cut to the quick. Gossip destroys character and is not edifying. As I write this, I'm painfully aware of my own shortcomings in this area. I have a strong sense of justice. When I see individuals wronged or slandered, it makes my blood boil. Sometimes it takes me to the point of saying things that later I may regret. Deeply.

So how do we strike a balance?

And what does the Bible have to say about disputes between friends, colleagues, husbands and wives? Well, one of the first principles should be speed. In Ephesians 4:26 Paul says, *'Don't let the sun go down while you're still angry.'* In 1 Corinthians 1:10 he exhorts us to *'live in harmony with each other. Let there be no divisions in the church.'* Proverbs 18:7 states it more plainly: *'The mouths of fools are their ruin, they trap themselves with their lips.'*

We have to be careful what we say, slow to anger and quick to say sorry. Please, please don't harbour grievances about wrongs that may – or may not – have been committed against you. They'll eat away at your soul. Do the right thing. Have it out with the person. Clear the air and try to do it in a loving manner. Soon. If you feel that's too difficult, find a third party, a mutual friend with no agenda, who can mediate and help you find a way through.

After all, that's *exactly* why Jesus came to earth. Isn't it?

As the Nike ad says, 'Just Do It'.

> **NICK'S NOTES**
>
> ✔ FIND A FRIEND WITH WHOM YOU CAN BE HONEST.
>
> ✔ FIND A WAY THROUGH YOUR HURTS.
>
> ✔ FIND SOMEONE WHO NEEDS YOUR HELP TO OVERCOME THEIR BITTERNESS.

6

ORANGES

'They are like trees planted along the riverbank, bearing fruit each season. Their leaves never wither, and they prosper in all they do.'
(Psalm 1:3)

Wouldn't it be terrible if there was only one fruit to eat? Yet sometimes church leaders are so frightened of other fruits, they upset the applecart just to keep the one they recognize, that makes them feel safe. When people come to know Jesus and churches grow through real confessions of faith, it's a wonderfully rewarding – if challenging – time.

> The church is the only army where the leaders shoot their own soldiers

As with the oak tree, sometimes an acorn will fall to the ground and a new tree will rise up. If they're wise, the leaders will tend to this plant, encourage, water and feed it. The new tree may not grow in the same way as its parent, but it has the same lineage. It should be birthed in grace and prayer and showered with the Holy Spirit.

Sadly, that's not always the case. All too frequently, man intervenes – and insecurity and jealousy can raise their ugly heads. The church is the only army where the leaders shoot their own soldiers. They don't mean to . . . they just do it out of fear. If somebody or something doesn't fit the mould or vision, then a walloping great emotional Exocet missile is let off in the lives of the perpetrators. This causes division, and people's hearts, lives and faith can be shaken to the core.

That's not the choreography of the Holy Spirit, but the destructive behaviour of people lost in the cant, rhetoric and polemic of a vision that must be followed at all costs. The body count can be massive. The wounds may take years to heal.

The **wounds** may take years to heal

At this point, the cauldron of gossip that has been simmering away nicely may well start to boil over. Wise men and women will still their tongues and pray, fast and intercede. What next? Well, all I know is, 'The battle belongs to the Lord.'

He will have the victory – not us mere mortals with our own selfish agendas, but God. Put on the full armour of God and pray as though your life depends on it.

It does.

NICK'S NOTES

✔ DON'T BE FRIGHTENED OF NEW THINGS.

✔ REMEMBER TO SAY SORRY.

✔ IF YOU HAVE A GRIEVANCE OR FEEL YOU'VE BEEN WRONGED, DON'T DELAY. SORT IT.

✔ FORGIVENESS IS THE KEY.

7

STEP TO IT?

'The family of the godly stands firm.'
(Proverbs 12:7)

What does 'family' mean these days? There are so many one-parent families struggling – emotionally, financially and spiritually. There are new families being welded together from the framework of previous relationships. The man brings his kids along and the woman brings hers and then – as if by magic – before long the inevitable happens and they have a child together.

Trust me, I know about this one.

Also, what does everybody call each other? I hate the word

> What does **'family'** mean these days?

'stepmother' – as do my children. But technically, that's the correct term for my new wife Nicky. She carries *immensely* more significance than that – at many levels. Aside from being my wonderful wife and partner, she's also the mother figure my children go to when they need to talk through stuff that they don't want to tell me just yet, or certain information that they know would freak me out!

She can never replace my late wife as their mum, and would never presume to. And yet 'stepmother' sounds a bit derogatory. In the end, my daughters decided to call her 'Smum', which stands for 'Second Mum'. But as they've matured, most of the time now they just call her Nicky.

And what of our new arrival – our son Jesse, born on 22 June 2008? Well, I don't give a fig about what he 'technically' might be. As far as we're all concerned, he's Misha and Jodie's much-prayed-for, long-awaited brother.

But it's hard, isn't it?

Don't shun 'Billy No Mates'

Because whatever we may all be happy with, other people – relatives and friends, particularly when there has been a significant former relationship – may view things very differently. From my own perspective, I remember with great love my father's second wife. It didn't matter to me one bit that we weren't from the same bloodline – nor did it matter to her. She made my dad immensely happy in their twenty-six-year marriage. She was a fabulous friend, and like an elder sister to me. We all miss her still.

So I don't think it's about 'blood is thicker than water'. That's not been my experience. It's about love – Christ-like, unconditional love (on a good day). It's also about grace as we seek to manage our new extended families, and about inviting people in. Be inclusive. Don't shun 'Billy No Mates' as he sits in your workplace, office, pub – or wherever you may be.

Welcome people. We're all part of God's family. And if it's to keep growing, then so must we, so that we can keep on blessing others. Ironically, the happy by-product is that we're also blessed in the process.

Result!

Family life can be a tricky business. But God has given us the rulebook – ten rules for a great life.

Let's do our best to stick to them and by them.

Rude not to.

> **NICK'S NOTES**
>
> ✔ KEEP IN TOUCH WITH YOUR EXTENDED FAMILY.
> ✔ SUPPORT ANY ELDERLY RELATIVES YOU MIGHT HAVE – EVEN JUST POPPING ROUND OCCASIONALLY IS APPRECIATED.
> ✔ YOU MIGHT BE THE ONLY FAMILY THAT SOMEONE ELSE HAS. . . .

8

SUFFER THE CHILDREN

'Your brother and your partner in suffering.'
(Revelation 1:9)

Just where is God? Three months ago, I set out to write what I thought were twelve inspiring stories of faith, hope and commitment. Then last week I found myself at a funeral for an eight-year-old child who'd been ill more or less from birth. I realized it's far too big a subject to be covered by twelve bite-sized, user-friendly, inspiring – yet palatable – chapters.

> Faith is believing in something we can't see

The truth is, at times it's been unpalatable.

So where is he? A young child dies. It's unfair. It's unjust. Sure, we can talk about how he'll have no more sorrow, no more pain, now he's with his Saviour. But in the circumstances, that can sound glib.

Why didn't he get that pain relief in this earthly life? Where was God then? In the hopes and prayers of his parents? In the hearts of their friends and community? If it's one of life's 'mysteries', and if our God is so great, why doesn't he show us and explain?

I know the answers – or at least some of 'em.

Faith is believing in something we can't see. And I do. You know, for thirty-six years now I have trusted in somebody I have yet to see, who I occasionally hear from, and whose timing and sense of humour never quite seem to match my own. I have endured much loss and heartache. I have also survived. On occasions, I can even be found bouncing in a Tigger-like joyful state round the environs of Chorleywood.

What have I learned, albeit reluctantly?

Just this. I know *very* little. I simply have to trust. Take that away, and in all honesty, I'd be up the creek without a paddle. I don't know why dreadful and tragic circumstances hit us. But we all experience them from time to time. Maybe it's just life and it happens to be your turn. I do know this, though. I would rather walk those painful miles shoulder-to-shoulder within a Christ-like loving community than not.

I know *very* little. I simply have to trust

And yes, God knows what goes on and why – because he's infinitely smarter than I'll *ever* be. It's just that I'd like a few more clues in this earthly life than I'm presently detecting. Is that a bad thing – to question things now and again, and not just blindly accept? Isn't that the nature of a proper adult relationship? You don't always understand why your partner does something, but you choose to carry on loving them anyway.

And isn't that what God does for us?

Full, frank, honest conversation. You can't beat it.

> **NICK'S NOTES**
>
> ✔ SPEND TIME WITH THOSE WHO ARE SUFFERING – IT WILL DO THEM, AND YOU, THE WORLD OF GOOD.
>
> ✔ TAKE TIME TO THINK OF THOSE WHO ARE SUFFERING IN DISTANT LANDS, AND PRAY FOR THEM.
>
> ✔ IF YOU ARE SUFFERING RIGHT NOW, HOLD ON, AND KNOW THAT BY HIS VERY NATURE, GOD CANNOT STOP LOVING YOU.

9

THE BOYFRIEND

*'He took the children in his arms
. . . and blessed them.'*
(Mark 10:16)

The words were like a dagger to my soul. 'Dad, how do you feel about me having a boyfriend?' said my 14-year-old daughter just the other day. My daughter – have a *boyfriend*? How *very* dare you! No man can ever be worthy enough, as far as I'm concerned!

I harrumphed a bit and slunk off to my study to look up the price of shotguns on eBay and check out the largest, most ferocious dog I could buy. Meanwhile, my wife Nicky delved a little deeper as the girls sat round the dining-table.

> My daughter – have a *boyfriend*?
> How *very* dare you!

Seriously, though, I'm glad that she felt able to even ask the question, and that she felt the lines of communication were still open. A little later, I returned to my seat, just in time to hear my wife say, 'What's he like?'

'Well, he goes to my school. He's English, but his mum and dad are Jamaican. I think he's two years older than me – and he's a Christian.'

I wasn't wild about him being older, I have to admit. I know only too well the way the male teenage mind works. After all, I was that spotty little Herbert, too. But they do say girls mature faster than boys, so . . . later on, Nicky and I suggested that she should invite him round for lunch whenever she liked. A few days later, 'he' arrived. He'd had a haircut especially for the occasion and was at first terribly shy.

> I slunk off to my study to look up the price of shotguns on eBay

I tentatively but *very* firmly shook his hand and said, 'Now, Peter, let's get the difficult stuff out of the way, shall we?'

A hush fell across the kitchen table. My eldest daughter rolled her eyes. The youngest stared at the floor. My wife, who is used to such monkey business, sighed.

'Which football team do you support?' I asked.

'Arsenal,' he replied.

'Well, my friend, we're definitely going to have to pray about that!'

He was gentle and polite. Both he and my daughter barely touched their lunch. I had a quiet word with him, and asked him how long he'd been a Christian and what his story was. He didn't hold back. And neither did I. My wife and I told them both that as long as they adhered to the boundaries laid down in the Bible – respecting each other and honouring God – we would support their friendship.

Was that maybe . . . a little heavy handed?

I like to think of it as the iron fist in the velvet glove. Later that day, as they walked down to the train station, Peter did the right and proper thing and asked my youngest daughter to be his girlfriend. It would have been rude not to.

In all honesty, given what goes on between young teenagers today, I think as parents we had a result. So much inappropriate stuff is going down, you wouldn't believe it. The innocence of the nation's youth is being eroded faster than Rooney can score for Man United. Bamboozled by dodgy pop videos, violent computer games, playground drugs and disgusting text messages, our kids are in desperate need of safe places. Home has to be where the heart is. So as hard as it might be, let's dig in for our kids. In many ways I suspect they're under far more pressure – at a far earlier age – than we ever were.

Laugh with them, listen to them, love them and pray for them.

It's all about the next generation.

NICK'S NOTES

✔ TAKE AN INTEREST IN YOUR CHILDREN'S EVERYDAY LIVES.

✔ TAKE YOUR CHILDREN OUT FOR A TREAT.

✔ GET TO KNOW YOUR CHILDREN'S FRIENDS A LITTLE – SOMETIMES A LOT!

10

GRACE

'We have been given a brief moment of grace.'
(Ezra 9:8)

When God gave out grace, I was at the back of the queue, shouting, 'Pick me! Pick me!' You see, I need it more than anyone. Sadly, for reasons obviously best known to himself, he didn't grant me that luxury. And now I detest queues of any kind.

> I detest **queues** of any kind

For example, it's Friday night, you've left work early to get home and make the most of your weekend. The motorways are log-jammed. So you take an 'A' road – only to get stuck behind a tractor or lorry driver who's convinced he owns the entire carriageway. Then you notice the petrol light is winking at you and you're about to run out of fuel. You divert to your local Tesco or Asda to get the cheapest petrol you can find – and things get worse. You arrive and find the rest of the planet has opted to do exactly the same thing.

'Give me my life back!'

Congratulations! You'll now waste twenty valuable minutes of your life positioning your car in such a way that the geezer in his Porsche 911 doesn't nip in front of you. He's rich, he's handsome, and a right flash git – with a pneumatic blonde wearing a very expensive little black dress perched à la mode beside him. Oh yes, he can wait.

Right?

The other thing that hacks me off is queuing to pay for your groceries in supermarkets. You know the kind of thing. There you are, one of seven people waiting to give your hard-earned cash to Tesco, Lidl, Morrisons or whoever, and they seem intent on delaying the process. There are three tills empty and unmanned – while the queue (ten items or less) gets ever longer behind you. Then you start to count how many items the little old lady in front of you has in her bulging basket. Twenty-seven! She shouldn't be here! Help!

The queue has now started to look like an evolutionary chain, and some shoppers are so knackered, they have the stoop of a Neanderthal to match. Pretty soon, unless something drastic happens, I'm going to start swinging from the rafters like the simian I am, boiling over with rage and demanding compensation.

'Give me my life back! You're stealing my time! How very dare you!'

Right?

Wrong.

Grace.

Yes, it's something you might remember from school, associated with food and feeling good: 'For what we are about to receive etc. . . .' But it's so much more than that. It's going the extra mile for someone. It's preferring the other person's needs to our own (being an only child, I've often struggled with that one!). It's smiling when we lose, congratulating the winner and meaning it. It's actively seeking to bless – often when you feel you've been dumped on from a great height and are subsequently swimming in elephant dung. It's trying to see the big picture. It's running the race and finishing well.

If you win, great. But did you *enjoy* running? Was it fun? In grace I believe we can find release. Grace gives us a certain freedom. The grace of God, on a good day when I'm tuned in properly . . . now that's totally awesome.

NICK'S NOTES

✔ TRY TO GIVE IN GRACEFULLY.

✔ PRAY FOR INCREASED PATIENCE WITH PORSCHE OWNERS – AND THEIR LIKE.

✔ THANK PEOPLE WHEN THEY SHOW GRACE TO YOU.

11

BREASTS

'Live happily with the woman you love.'
(Ecclesiastes 9:9)

I know what you're thinking. How can he possibly write about those? I mean, we all love them, but surely he's not going to go there! Isn't that completely out of order for a bloke who's meant to be following God?

I should say right at the outset of this homage to the 'twin peaks' of the female form, I have no

I think we're pre-programmed to admire them

intention of being crude or salacious. Rather, like many famous poets from King Solomon to Leonard Cohen, I have come to understand my fascination and love of them.

It starts right from the word 'go'. And I believe it's inherently God-given. As soon as we're born, we start looking around for them. I've watched my baby son Jesse do just that. It took him a couple of days before he got the hang of 'latching on'. But once he'd cracked it – ably abetted by his mum and dad – there was no turning back. For him, they're a source of great comfort, warmth and nourishment. And even if you weren't breast fed as a child, mum's chest was always a warm and safe place.

Is it any wonder that as men we continue to find them . . . fascinating?

And let's be really honest here. I think we're pre-programmed to admire them. No – I'm not talking about being like some pervy bloke in a dodgy raincoat or the office pest who just ogles and stares. That's plainly unacceptable – it's sexual harassment. This is something else. I'm talking about saying quietly to yourself, 'Thank you, God, for your marvellous creation.' You see, we can look and appreciate – but it's the thought process and integrity of it that really matters.

Breasts are beautiful

I don't agree with the way the female form is paraded in lads' mags, tabloids and top-shelf titles. For me, that kind of display objectifies and degrades women. And don't give me all that *shinola* – that the girls are emancipated, love their work and feel good about what they're doing. Ask yourself – what are those images really used for?

You see, I think it's possible to really love and appreciate women in all their splendour. But as Jesus says, *'If your eye causes you to sin . . .'* I know, it sounds like a tough command in these lax, liberal days. Yet it boils down to one simple thing. Love one woman. Appreciate women and the female form but – and this is a big 'but' – keep it pure.

Breasts are beautiful. Let's keep them that way.

> **NICK'S NOTES**
>
> ✔ KEEP YOUR THOUGHTS PURE.
>
> ✔ ENCOURAGE RIGHT THINKING.
>
> ✔ DON'T BE AFRAID TO PROTEST WHEN YOU SEE SOMETHING THAT IS WRONG.

12

A PINT, A PUB AND A PRAYER

'Encourage the young men to live wisely.'
(Titus 2:6)

It was the American writer Flannery O'Connor who wrote *A Good Man is Hard to Find*. Later, Maria McKee extrapolated this in a song called 'A Good Heart is Hard to Find', and Feargal Sharkey made it into a hit.

But is it true?

Is a good man hard to find? I'm not sure he is. I think it may be hard to find men who are prepared to open up and be vulnerable, but they do exist. And why aren't we seeing more of these men in church? Well, I think we have to face the fact that many of them think of church as cold, lifeless and dull. Men are also put off by church being a bit 'girly' with lots of 'I love you' songs about God. I think men want something – dare I say it? – more ballsy.

So where do they head? Well, somewhere that's warm, welcoming and where people won't ask too many difficult questions. Well, OK, maybe stuff about football and what formation you think Alex

Ferguson might use this forthcoming Saturday, and perhaps some idle speculation about whether the barmaid looks like Catherine Zeta-Jones or Keira Knightley. There's a world of difference, after all. But mainly it's a haven of rest from the rigours of life. Tarry too long, though, and you'll be so laid back you'll be horizontal.

> many men think of church as cold

They don't call it Theakston's Old Peculiar for nothing. But it's here that a lot of men will go to find solace and safety, friendship and even a sense of community and belonging. Here they can brag about their new car, their girlfriend, and their latest technological gadget – the size of their widget and other things men hold dear. What they won't do, unless they're three sheets to the wind, is tell you what breaks their heart, why they're not at home with their families and why they'd rather sit in the snug than snuggle up to the wife.

When I was younger, I used to try to escape my responsibilities from time to time. But it's a hiding to nothing. Jesus' life was a walk of selflessness, not self*ish*ness, and we're called to try to do the same. But how did I get to work all this through? Well, it started back in 1993 when we first moved into Chorleywood and the phone rang one evening. We'd just completed our daughter Misha's bath-time and were in the process of putting her to bed.

'Hi, my name's Alan,' a strange voice said. 'I'm from St Andrews and wondered if you played football?'

'It's been quite some time,' I answered. 'Do you fancy a pint instead?'

From that one phone call, a wonderful friendship blossomed that endures to this day. At the pub, we slowly opened up and traded confidences, and over time did some serious life miles together. I became godfather to his son. Later, when my mother lay dying at Royal Hallamshire Hospital, Sheffield, it was Alan who sat outside the room praying while I went to be with her. He does what it says on the tin. Alan was – and is – a real man. Like me, he gets a lot of things wrong. Yet he had the courage to respond to God nudging him.

There are real men in the Bible, too – like David, who sent Uriah into the front line of battle, thus ensuring that he would die, so that David could have his way with Uriah's wife. Yet there's no doubt that David was a man of God – even though, like the rest of us, he was 'deeply flawed'. Abraham was impatient to father a great nation, so he slept with Hagar the maid, who wasn't his wife – not the smartest thing to do, was it? I'm not suggesting you emulate these men, but you can see they were all too human. Sin is part of our DNA. However, thank God we know we have a forgiving Saviour. If I didn't have Jesus in my life, I'd be so far up the creek without a paddle, I'd have excavated something the size of Wookey Hole in the side of Mount Everest.

Thank goodness God operates despite men. Let me tell you a true story. . . .

A while back I was booked to speak at a men's supper. It was the middle of winter and involved a long drive, and I wasn't looking forward to it – partly, if I'm honest, because they'd said up front they didn't really have any money to pay me – but also because I'd rather have been at home with my family. So I was in a great big sulk. This was not improved when my friend James came round to pray with me.

'Mate, I think you may well find three men tonight who are all dealing with a very deep sense of loneliness,' he said.

I can remember thinking, *One of them will be me – because I could be cuddling up to my wife on the sofa*. So off I travelled to the borders of Sussex, and after a couple of hours I arrived at a tiny village pub. I found a bunch of highly intellectual academics and City types with names like Charles Barking Bowles and the Very Reverend Quentin Roger-Nightly. I began to speak, and felt nothing was working. Nobody laughed where they usually did. The overall feel of the room was very stiff and forbidding. A lot of the men were clearly very uncomfortable with my testimony – particularly when I described my late wife's cancer journey. By the time I got to the end of my talk, I was relieved to have made it. Yet afterwards I was left with three men in front of me. As fed up as I was, I had to chuckle at God's ingenuity and faithfulness.

Real men stuff up

The first man had lost his dad in a car accident at the age of 13, and he'd never dealt with it. He was approaching 50. The second man had a father who had only worked nights, and he was grieving over the lack of relationship with his dad because he had no happy childhood memories. The third – and most reticent – told me his dad had left when he was 6, and as a result of my talk, he was going to try to find him before it was too late. He was 50 and his dad would be in his seventies. I prayed for each of them and felt humbled. Why? Well, because God took my flawed, ungrateful, resentful heart and not only used me but also blessed me – despite my lack of grace.

Finally, when I thought I'd finished, an older gentleman came up to me. He said he had lost his wife and had somehow endured that. But he then told me about his daughter, who had cancer. The time came for her to leave the hospice so she could die peacefully at home. However, on arrival she said to her dad, 'I've got to go back.'

'Why?' he asked.

'Because there's a man there who's promised to come to the Alpha course – but he hasn't signed up.'

This beautiful woman was taken back. The man signed up. And she came home and went to be with the Lord. How faithful she was in her journey! And how confident she was of her inheritance, to spend some of her last precious minutes trying to make sure this man would come to Christ.

At the end of the evening, I picked up the coins they'd thrown into a plastic pot for me and looked at them. And then I looked at my heart. I felt – and I still feel – like a millionaire to have been there as these men shared their treasures of darkness in a pub. And I realized this was *their* church.

Real men stuff up. It's what we do. We're found in all the wrong places, hopefully at the right time. But God, through his Son, redeems us in the most extraordinary ways. We need to reach these men – as well as the women. If they won't come to a church because of stereotypical images like 'people use church as a crutch', then we have to take church to them. Keep it informal.

We need to move up and out in order to keep growing. And for me that's about genuine friendship, living out the love of Jesus in our communities. It's all about a pint, a pub and a prayer. What God can start in a man's heart can affect thousands for generations to come.

Let's accept that we're imperfect – but let's not shirk our responsibilities.

I'll have a pint of John Smith's, please.

> **NICK'S NOTES**
>
> ✔ FOOTBALL AND FOAMING ALE CAN BE A GREAT COMBINATION.
>
> ✔ DON'T BE AFRAID TO WELCOME YOUR NEIGHBOUR.

13

HORSES

'Turn the horses and get me out of here!'
(1 Kings 22:34)

It won't make me popular with some sections of our local community. But one thing that really gets my goat is this – people riding horses on roads designed for much faster traffic. They saunter along, happily clip-clopping away, while we drive at five miles an hour behind, waiting for them to deign to acknowledge our presence. Then they gaily wave us by as if we've been granted some special permission or gift, all the time smiling benignly in a *Stepford Wives* fashion. The ultimate irony is to watch them negotiate a speed bump!

> Perhaps they should have some kind of **giant** equine nappy for **catching the dung**

When you finally make it home, and manage to park your car in your drive, they'll clip-clop by half an hour later and stop right outside – while their horse leaves you a nice steaming present by your front door. As a dog owner, I have to sweep up my pet's waste products, so why can't people who ride horses do the same? Perhaps they should have some kind of giant equine nappy for catching the dung. Let's see how many Tabithas and Quentins would be riding horses then!

As we're on this subject, a while back a friend of ours – who happens to be a Maasai warrior from Kenya – came for lunch. We thought we'd show him a little bit of our village life, and took him up to the common with our dog Max. As soon as our little canine chum had performed his party trick, we gingerly placed the offending item into a nappy sack while our Maasai friend looked on amazed.

'This is a very strange country you live in,' he said.

My wife and I pondered on this later in the day. We had to agree. If you're from Kenya and used to wide open spaces, you're probably not going to spend your time clearing up after a herd of wildebeest, now, are you?

After all, it would be a lifetime's work – and I think we're called to do something much more worthwhile.

NICK'S NOTES

✔ ON OCCASIONS BE PREPARED TO CLEAR UP OTHER PEOPLE'S MESS.

14

CRADLE TO THE GRAVE

'Godliness makes a nation great.'
(Proverbs 14:34)

Time was, when you opened a bank account, you would establish a relationship that would last for many years and, in some cases, for life. We used such phrases as, 'My word is my bond.' Back then it meant something. There was a genuine sense of doing the right thing by people, and of being accountable.

Now it seems that bankers, fat cats, rich kids – call 'em what you like (erm . . . maybe not!) – can mismanage our money, and when it all goes sour, they can walk off with a redundancy package of many millions of pounds/dollars. One person allegedly walked away with £160 million. Just what did they do to deserve such a golden handshake?

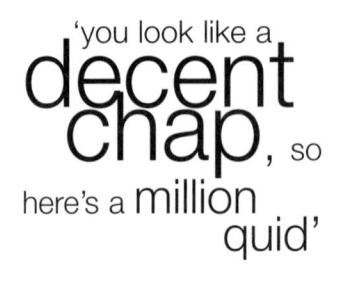

'you look like a **decent chap**, so here's a **million quid**'

That must be incredible! Imagine stuffing up royally at work. Your boss calls you in. 'Well, Reginald, since you've been here,' he says, 'the goods our customers ordered have never arrived on time – and in some cases haven't arrived at all. And it appears this has been going on for quite some time – in fact, I believe, for over five years now. So I'm afraid we're going to have to let you go. But you look like a decent chap, so here's a million quid.'

Insane, isn't it?

And yet this kind of moral turpitude still goes on. When he's not busy removing the daggers and arrows from his back – courtesy of his own party – Gordon Brown (Prime Minister at the time of writing) has been doing his level best to sort this out. Given his childhood and background, you'd think he'd have a stronger sense of justice than most. Yet it appears we're at the mercy of the world's economy – and in particular the economies of the USA and South-East Asia.

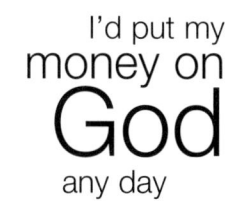

> I'd put my money on God any day

What a frightening thought.

We desperately need to pray for the likes of Obama and his colleagues, 'running' the US of A. On present evidence, they and us are in dire need of supernatural help from the ultimate saver and Saviour. One of Matt Redman's songs asks, 'Can A Nation Be Changed?' Well, I don't know, but I do know this – we can't afford to stop praying or stop trying.

And I'd put my money on God any day.

I can't afford not to.

NICK'S NOTES

✔ BET ON GOD AND BACK A WINNER.

✔ PRAY FOR OUR POLITICAL LEADERS, AND PRAY FOR OUR NATION AND ALL NATIONS TO BE FINANCIALLY HEALTHY.

✔ PRAY FOR BARACK OBAMA, ONE OF THE MOST POWERFUL MEN IN THE WORLD.

15

GOLDEN SLUMBERS

'So the L<small>ORD</small> God caused the man to fall into a deep sleep.'
(Genesis 2:21)

In my waking hours, of which there are currently many, I dream of sleep – per chance even to dream! But for the past few nights, there's been more chance of hell freezing over, my losing three stone, or Jeremy Clarkson quietly admitting he likes to go to the ballet occasionally while wearing his wife's pink fluffy slippers. With my advancing years, I thought I'd have less energy but more patience. I'm rather disappointed to say I'm not sure that's true.

I'm one of the most **selfish** people you could ever wish *not* to meet.

I love my son. I'm *incredibly* grateful to God for the wonder of his being here at all. It's just that deep down, there still lurks 'The Only Child'. Honestly, I'm one of the most selfish people you could ever wish *not* to meet. Oh, I do my best to disguise it. I've become so adept at it, on occasions my selfishness blends so chameleon-like into the environment that most people can hardly tell it's there. But sometimes it bursts forth, often with rapier-like coruscating wit, of which I am rarely proud.

Let's take today. I was woken at 3.30 a.m. by our little lad demanding his breakfast. I tossed and turned for three more hours, pummelled by any stupid thing that could come into my brain to taunt me and prevent me drifting off to the gentle land of nod. The result? At 6.30 I got up, as I always do, to take my youngest daughter to school. But this time I felt like a cup of cold sick. (I should perhaps make it clear that I didn't *want* a cup of cold sick. I just *felt* like one . . . No, that doesn't sound any better. Move on, Nick . . .)

Anyway, to cut a very long story short, my wife and I ended up in a kids' shop trying to buy an outfit for our son's christening. It was at this point that an innate reverse sexism took over, as the lady who owned the shop was helpful and kind – but her conversation was directed *very clearly* at my wife and not at me. To make matters worse, a customer opined her point of view while I silently tried to maintain my cool. When she made it her business for the fourth time to suggest just what my son should wear, the dam burst. Without any time for the editing process to kick in, I blurted out:

'I'll tell you what! Would you like me to come round to your house and tell you how to decorate your lounge?'

For a minute she looked stunned. But she had enough nous and humour to fire back:

'Well, I can say what I like, 'cos you can't divorce me! I'm not your wife!'

We all laughed in an embarrassed fashion. A few minutes later I found enough *politesse* to say, 'Bye – thanks very much! You're not shy, are you?'

'And neither are you!' she retorted.

Our verbal version of *It's A Knockout* complete, I limped out of the shop feeling like John Wayne after he's been attacked by the bad guys. I didn't even have time to circle the wagons. I really must learn not to have the last word, not to be the spoilt child – just because I can be. And anyway, who really wins in these situations?

> I need a great big mug of 'Shut up!'

I can't remember who it was who said, 'Patience is a virtue seldom found in women and never in men!' But they might well have been on to something. I need to rest more in God and not in myself. I need to seek his face and have greater wisdom and patience. And an early night might be a sound idea.

Oh, and one more thing: I need a great big mug of 'Shut up!'

NICK'S NOTES

✔ BEWARE OF BECOMING A SPOILT CHRISTIAN.

✔ BEWARE OF YOUR SHARP RESPONSES.

✔ BEWARE OF INSOMNIA.

16

MOTORBIKIN'

'His chariots are like whirlwinds.'
(Jeremiah 4:13)

I remember it well. It was 49cc of metallic red-and-chrome heaven. It was my Motobecane Mobylette Sports moped. It had a small dent in the petrol tank – not my doing – which had enabled my dad to negotiate a much better deal when he purchased it. As my parents divorced, my bike gave me much greater freedom to come and go wherever I liked – often with a wide variety of musical instruments strapped to me or my mean machine.

> Doctors and nurses in hospitals refer to 'bikers' and their ilk as 'donors'

It wasn't particularly fast or reliable (it was designed and built by the French, after all!), but it was my first real whiff of danger. On a downhill run with a following wind (none of it mine, I hasten to add) it could reach 50 miles an hour. It could often be unpredictable on ice or in a snowstorm. OK, let's be honest here – it could be downright dangerous. I still have a twinge in my shoulder when I think about it. But it was tremendous fun, if a bit chilly at times.

However, on turning 17, I didn't feel inclined to progress to a bigger, faster model – but opted instead for four wheels as opposed to two.

Doctors and nurses in hospitals refer to 'bikers' and their ilk as 'donors'. Although that appeals to my sense of humour, the reality is stark and brutal. If you have a bike, it will only be a matter of time before you fall off. I promise.

Do I sound like a boring old fart?

So if you're still set on having a mean machine – a Triumph, a BSA or, worst of all, a Hog (they're American and, in my book, strictly for girls) – please get equipped with the right boots and leathers and go on an advanced driving course.

I still get upset when people on motorbikes seem to have scant regard for their personal safety. They put themselves and other road users seriously at risk, undertaking on and off motorways, often at great speed. Do I sound like a boring old fart? Well if do, sorry, but the statistics back me up.

As for other road users like me, it has to be . . .

Think once. Think twice. Think bike.

NICK'S NOTES

✔ BE AWARE.

✔ PRAY FOR SAFETY BEFORE YOU TURN ON THE IGNITION.

17

PRAYER POWER

'Accept my prayer as incense offered to you.'
(Psalm 141:2)

I believe wholeheartedly in the power of prayer. But I'm here to tell you God doesn't always answer our supplications the way we'd like – or in a way we understand. Often we can see with more clarity looking back. But I don't feel we'll ever truly understand in this life. I also wonder how many times we need to ask him for things. Does he ever get fed up with our nagging him – instead of trusting him and believing he heard us in the first instance? Or is it simply our human condition?

> Does God ever get **fed up** with our **nagging** him?

We worry. We look for obvious dramatic signs – thunderbolts, spiritual or otherwise. But most of the time it doesn't work like that. Of course, it's enormously positive for groups of people to pray and seek God's guidance – and I also feel it's imperative to pray for the sick. But at what point, if any, should we stop and simply . . . trust?

I'm not saying that we should abandon responsible attitudes and accountability in our prayer life. But maybe we should think about this. When I fell over as a little boy, I used to run to my mum or dad, and they would cuddle me, reassure me and fix me up with sticking plasters or whatever I needed. Instinctively, they knew when they heard my cry that I was hurt. They didn't need to hear it a second time to come running. If mortal parents are like that, how much more does our heavenly Father hear us when we're hurting, lost, distressed or frightened?

> I chose to believe, and still do, that in his infinite wisdom, God knows best

Yet at times it can be excruciatingly painful. When my first wife was fighting cancer, we had shed-loads of prayer – all-night vigils, healing services and more. God's ears must have been burning and his in-tray overflowing on her behalf. We threw everything we could at the ugly disease in our own strength – yes, in our human weakness – but also we begged God for mercy.

But it didn't happen.

Or did it? God heard our prayers and the cry of many hearts – and especially those of my children and, indeed, their mother. And in the end, he answered our prayers with a severe mercy. Her suffering stopped.

He took her home.

And here's where the rubber meets the road. When the stuff hits the fan like that, do you choose to go on believing – or do you give up? It's easy to do the latter and become bitter and cynical, and yet what a dreadful waste that would be. I chose to believe, and still do, that in his infinite wisdom, God knows best.

I don't always like what he does. I'm frequently at odds with him. But the God of the moon and stars – who made us all and this planet we're trying very hard not to mess up – has to know best.

Got more questions than answers?

Pray.

It doesn't matter when, where or how. You don't have to be eloquent. Just call out to God in your own special way. It's the only way I know.

> **NICK'S NOTES**
>
> ✔ DON'T BE CYNICAL. GOD HEARS OUR CRY.
> ✔ DON'T GIVE UP. HE WILL SOMEHOW SUSTAIN YOU.

18

SPIN OR SIN?

'Truth springs up from the earth.'
(Psalm 85:11)

I guess when we ruminate on some of the greatest exponents of spin in recent years, we'd have to consider Alastair Campbell as the doyen of the culture.

But what is spin, actually?

Is it the propagation of rumour, scandal and heresy? Or is it the equally dark art of almost telling the truth but never quite getting round to it? You know the kind of thing – presidents who don't lie, but are economical with the truth and the whereabouts of little things like weapons of mass destruction. And then there's the sublime humour of the oxymoron. On my way to a speaking engagement the other day, I passed a sign saying, 'Secret Nuclear Bunker'. How can it possibly be a secret if there's a whopping great signpost showing you which way to go?

I'm all for full, frank conversation

Sometimes it's what we don't say that's as damaging as what we do – such as when people craftily allude to a person and a particular circumstance without ever actually saying what they did wrong. For example, 'He's been an amazing pillar of the church, but is a bit of a maverick.' What should we deduce from that? He's faithful but not good at following orders? He's a lovely bloke but he's fallen out with the clergy? Was he muttering about defrocking the vicar under his breath? Or did he simply have a different view to the vision of the Reverend Walter Wearisome and his curate Edna Trifle?

We'll never know.

So what's the point in covertly besmirching someone? I'm all for full, frank conversation. Let's get it all out in the open. Dare to seek out the truth. Explore what you're told. Don't just take it as (sic) gospel. The louder and longer somebody protests that it is, in my experience that usually means it isn't.

And if you feel that someone – be it the media, your boss, a local MP, or (heaven forefend) your church – is bowling you a googly, don't be afraid to step up to the crease and knock it for six. A long time ago a young man did just that in the temple in Jerusalem. He caused quite a stink.

Fair play to him.

The truth is like a light to all darkness.

Ultimately it will always prevail.

NICK'S NOTES

✔ KNOW WHEN TO ASK A DIFFICULT QUESTION.

✔ PRAY FOR DISCERNMENT.

✔ DO YOUR LEVEL BEST NOT TO GET SELF-RIGHTEOUS ABOUT IT. (I REALLY STRUGGLE WITH THIS ONE!)

19

IN GOD'S NAME?

'You made a great name for yourself when you redeemed your people . . .'
(2 Samuel 7:23)

Among the enduring disappointments in my life are the things that get said and done in God's name. Holy wars, for instance. I mean, what kind of nonsense is that?

> Holy wars
> – I mean, what kind of
> **nonsense**
> is that?

I've come to the sad conclusion that God uses the broken and the dysfunctional – and even the downright bitter – for his glory and purpose. And as one of his mortal jars of clay, I can see quite clearly that he does stuff in spite of me.

Oh yes, I can be a stubborn man when I see justice violated, or people slandered and reputations tarnished. It brings out the worst in me – especially when this happens within the church.

The classic, 'I really believe the Lord wants to go in this direction . . .' sketch is always a good one. It makes me want to say, 'If you *really* believe that to be true, then please weigh it, test it, and *pray* about it. Don't rush headlong into what could be disaster.' Do I sound over-cautious? Like a bit of a control freak? Well, let's own up here. I *am* a bit of a control freak, which is why (a) I can spot them a mile off, and (b) I try, on a daily basis, to give everything back to God.

You see, bright ideas, dreams and visions are all creative gifts – but it's how we interpret and use them that really matters. Maybe it's a lack of faith on my part, but it would be a brave man indeed who said either, 'God told me' or 'I believe it's the Lord's will'. I, for one, would be extremely worried in case I got it wrong or appeared to use his name in vain.

Somewhere far off in the distance, I can hear the ghost of Kenneth Williams shouting, 'Infamy, infamy, they've all got it in for me!'

NICK'S NOTES

✔ SEEK WISDOM.

✔ HAND THE REINS OVER TO GOD.

✔ TRY HARD NOT TO BE JUDGEMENTAL.

20

HEARTS AND BONES

'It's better to be a live dog than a dead lion!'
(Ecclesiastes 9:4)

My canine chum Max is fast approaching his twelfth birthday. He's started to become a little too obsessive. I know what you're thinking. I can hear you now: 'Well, they say dogs take after their owners!' The problem, simply put, is this. When my little pal gets a bit fed up or depressed, he starts to 'fettle' – as we'd say in Yorkshire. For some reason, he'll gnaw at himself until his feet are literally almost red raw.

I'm **not** a patient man – as my family will tell you

Thankfully, we've now learned to spot this act of canine flagellation. Then we sprint into the kitchen to fit what looks like a large funnel on his head to curb his instinct for self-chastisement (well, let's face it – he already has the hair shirt).

He'll also dig a hole for his chewy treat or bone and bury it in the garden. Sometimes it will lie there for months on end, before he exhumes it and gnaws away for hours until his work is done and it exists no more.

'What rot is he writing now?' I hear you thinking!

Well, you see, I can behave from time to time like my dog. No, I'm not talking about peeing on lamp-posts and sniffing strangers' bottoms. I'm more concerned about my inability to leave things alone instead of constantly carping on about them. I'm not a patient man – as my family will tell you – and can let things niggle me to the point of distraction. Just when I think I've dealt with it and put it all to bed, some trigger is set off in my over-active psyche and I'll dig up all the nastiness again. It's not good, is it?

What can I do?

Well, getting rid of the mental list of wrongdoings is a good way to start. If I keep shorter accounts with other people and myself, things might start to get a little easier. I may even choose to smile more.

I may not smile like Mona Lisa and I'm certainly not enigmatic.

But who wants to be a moaning mister?

> **NICK'S NOTES**
>
> ✔ LOOK UP THE WORD 'PEDANTIC' IN THE DICTIONARY AND THEN GIVE UP BEING A PLONKER!
>
> ✔ LOOK IN THE MIRROR. GOD LOVES YOU, SO YOU CAN'T BE THAT BAD!
>
> ✔ LAUGH AT YOUR OWN IDIOSYNCRASIES. LAUGHTER IS THE BEST MEDICINE.

21

STOP THE TRAFFIK

'You will break the yoke of their slavery.'
(Isaiah 9:4)

Our Jesse narrowly escaped being called 'Wilberforce'. That could've been his first name! Why? Well, because William Wilberforce is one of my heroes. He was a man who wasn't afraid to swim against the tide. He sacrificed his health, and at times his reputation, to pursue the path of righteous justice. He wouldn't give in and was relentless in his mission to abolish slavery. In the end – many years later – he succeeded.

here in the twenty-first century, **slavery** still goes on

So it's with great sadness that I acknowledge that here in the twenty-first century, slavery still goes on. And it goes something like this. Unscrupulous men befriend young women from poor countries and promise them a better life. But on arrival in the UK, the girls are imprisoned, sexually assaulted, and violated in ways you don't want to imagine. Then they're sent to work to pay off the so-called 'debt' for coming here in the first place.

Their pimps control their every movement. Quite often there will be a 'good cop' who appears kind but can turn quite nasty – as well as the ugly truth of the 'bad cop'. The girls are threatened that if they don't comply, they or their families will be attacked and, in some cases, murdered. Often they're controlled with drugs – legal or otherwise – to make them more malleable.

When the girls become too tired, too ill or too old, they are sold on like cattle to another, more 'downmarket' (if there is such a thing) trader in flesh. I cannot begin to imagine the misery these poor women have to endure. You may be wondering why I even write about it. The ugly truth is this. It's middle-class, educated men who frequent the brothels where these girls are kept. And those houses are often located in 'nice middle-class areas', not always on the wrong side of the tracks. There might well be one in your neighbourhood.

> I cannot begin to imagine the **misery** these poor **women** have to endure

Society has objectified women for far too long – through the magazines that parade on the top shelf and the tabloids that lie on the bottom shelf. So is it any wonder there are punters out there using women who've been forced into prostitution? Those men probably don't even realize the girls have been trafficked. And how would they? What are they going to do – sit down and have a nice cosy chat about how the girls are getting on in their job?

What does God have to say about injustice?

Well, he says, *'God, in his justice, will punish anyone who does such things'* (Romans 2:2). He also says, *'In his justice he will pay back those who persecute you'* (2 Thessalonians 1:6). That sounds good, doesn't it? So what can we do in earthly terms to help the oppressed?

The glib and easy answer is to pray. Phew, that lets us off the hook nicely, doesn't it? I can tick the box, having prayed, and relax knowing I've done my bit. That's the road I'm most likely to take. But it's the road less travelled we need to look at. We can start putting our time and money into lobbying politicians, challenging governments, being aware of other people who might be at risk – even helping, on occasions, to gather intelligence.

You see, for things to change, so that teenage girls are no longer being trafficked over borders and sold into misery, there has to be a build-up of public opinion. Only when that's at its peak and the kettle boils over, will we see real change. You can help, though. There is an excellent organization fighting this global crime. Please, if you have the time, check out their website – www.stopthetraffik.co.uk – and if you need any further inspiration, just look at your daughters or nieces.

I guarantee you'll want to make a difference.

> **NICK'S NOTES**
>
> ✔ YOU STAND UP FOR JESUS, WHEN YOU STAND UP FOR JUSTICE.
>
> ✔ PRAY FOR THE OPPRESSED AS WELL AS THEIR CAPTORS.
>
> ✔ DON'T STOP BELIEVING THAT ONE DAY WE WILL HAVE A FAIR SOCIETY.

22

THE FUNNY BONE

'Let everything you say be good and helpful.'
(Ephesians 4:29)

Over the past few years I have watched open-mouthed as broadcasting standards have plummeted, coarse language has become the new vernacular, and people's tawdry lives are paraded across our television screens as they gasp greedily for the oxygen that will give them five minutes of fame.

But does anybody know what's funny any more?

As a young man I used to lap up Morecambe and Wise's brilliant comic wit on the telly. On occasion, when allowed, I loved to watch the more oblique japes and jocularity that the superb *Monty Python* team created. But is it me, or has a dark cloud of vulgarity and ugly wit descended on us over the last twenty years? It seems modern comics struggle to get through their acts without swearing or

does anybody know **what's funny** any more?

blaspheming profusely. Whatever happened to a talent like Norman Wisdom's – who I once saw entertain an awards ceremony for five minutes just by his great sense of physical comedy and that grin of his? Tommy Cooper and Les Dawson were brilliant men who didn't resort to the lowest common denominator.

I have an idea.

I think language has become devalued

I think language has become devalued. If my dad ever said 'bloody hell', I knew it was *very* serious. But what used to be really shocking has now been replaced by the 'F' word. And now even that is becoming worn. The new taboo is the 'C' word. We're living in a society that needs to have its vocabulary serviced and its imagination expanded – and not through class 'A' drugs, which burn out, rather than boost, your brain cells. We're living in a society that, to my jaundiced eye, looks like a runaway horse about to leap into a very deep ravine.

What can we do?

Well, let's explore language. Don't settle for the easy option. Get creative. It can be fun, if occasionally painful. I remember as a pre-teen avidly devouring the 'Jennings' books written by Anthony Buckeridge. One of Jennings' favourite phrases was, 'Fossilized fish-hooks'. So, in all innocence, I used the phrase at a woodwork class when I clouted my thumb with a hammer. I was stunned – quite literally – when my teacher smacked me round the head.

'What did you do that for, sir?' I cried, reeling from his blow while trying to stem the crimson tide flowing from my thumb.

'We both know what that means, Battle. Do *not* use it again!'

In truth I didn't. But at a later date I found out. It seems that on that day my teacher had lost his funny bone.

> **NICK'S NOTES**
>
> ✔ TURN ON.
> ✔ TUNE IN.
> ✔ AND DROP OUT IF YOU DON'T LIKE WHAT YOU SEE OR HEAR.

23

THE CRITIC

'Always think carefully before pronouncing judgement.'
(2 Chronicles 19:6)

I've been asked to review records for a magazine. But it leaves me in a bit of a quandary. Just how honest should I be if I really detest something? As an artist – and a sensitive one at that – I'm very susceptible to criticism and frankly, not fond of it. In fact, I'm positively allergic!

> I'm very **susceptible** to **criticism** and frankly, not fond of it

However, I do hold strong opinions as to what is great music, good music and frankly awful music. Of course, it's only my opinion, and we all know how subjective we can be. But for the record, can America please stop exporting generic sound-alike Christian rock bands to the UK, with their enormodrome guitar riffs and attempts at meaningful lyrics? If I want to enjoy something so patently asinine, I can watch daytime television.

For the record (*sic*), songs should be life-enhancing, affirming paeans of praise to our Creator and those we love – not *sturm und drang* pomposity dressed up in a thin veneer of wannabe stadium rock, with the odd 'J' and 'G' word tossed in for good measure.

And yet there's a lot about Americans I love – such as the way they come up to you and say, 'How ya doin'?' – while positively oozing sincerity from every pore. Or the delicious way in which they *don't* do irony. For example, had I answered that question with, 'Well, why don't you pull up a chair and sit down and I'll tell you all about it,' in most cases that would be lost on them completely and they'd be genuinely puzzled.

They do love a good election, though. And for months now, we in the UK have been fed a diet of Obama's and McCain's recent movements. That is, right up until the former made history by achieving the dream that Martin Luther King died for and Jesse Jackson still believed in – and the latter went the way of all chips, into the waste disposal. Everyone – rich and poor, young and old – queued for hours to vote for their candidate.

As a result, America once again stands on the brink of a massive sea change – cultural, global and certainly financial. Let's hope Barack Obama has an easier time of it than some of his country's well-intentioned, well-meaning musical exports.

> **NICK'S NOTES**
>
> ✔ PRAY THAT THE PRES. DOES THE RIGHT THING.
>
> ✔ PRAY THAT I DO THE RIGHT THING.
>
> ✔ DON'T BECOME TOO POMPOUS!

24

MOTHERS

'From my mother's womb you have cared for me.'
(Psalm 71:6)

I've been thinking a lot about my mum, who passed away eleven years ago. It's kind of taken me a little by surprise, but I still really miss her. We didn't have the best of relationships – if I were to be unkind, I would say her closest one was arguably with a bottle. But she contributed at least 50 per cent of my DNA – certainly emotionally, and maybe spiritually, too.

> The mother/son **relationship** is a special one

In the end she sort of got alcoholic dementia. I'd ring the hospital ward and hear her screaming as she lost her mind. She was a member of Exit, the voluntary euthanasia society. I don't think she was ever terribly happy on this earth. (I've just read that back and realized the irony of that statement.)

There were pockets of sunshine – one relationship that brought her happiness for a while; her time spent as a Cub Scout leader; the early years of her marriage; and her own mum, my nana, who doted on her. She possessed a great sense of humour, and before she lost the plot, she had a wonderfully quick wit.

I guess having had our Jesse and having watched all the other grandparents' joy at his arrival, I feel my mum is missing out. Big time. But there are other questions, too. I watch how my wife holds him and plays with him, and I wonder if my mum was ever that tender with me. I look at my daughters and I'm curious about what life might have been like if I'd had siblings like them.

The mother/son relationship is a special one. I believe in many cases it's the model for how we relate to women. In my case, for most of my adult life, I struggled. I knew my mum loved me to bits, but I was also hugely aware of her weaknesses. Consequently, I sought to be in control, and at the first or second sign of weakness or instability – I was gone.

On two out of the three occasions when I've actually fallen in love in this life, it was with women who were strong, feisty and independent. Of course, that creates its own set of interesting dilemmas. By the third time, I'd done a bunch of life miles and not a little therapy, and hopefully I have had some of my hard edges chipped off. But my mum was sensitive, and I like to think that on a good day, I can be that as well. She gave me a love of music. She instilled in me a love of God through nightly prayers – a habit which she kept up long after I had left home.

> the best **parent** in the world is my heavenly Father

I have much to thank her for. Yet at times in my daily life – and in my autobiography *Big Boys Don't Cry* – I've been less than kind. Why is that? And will my son harbour dark thoughts about his mum or dad? I think it may have been the poet Philip Larkin who said, 'They **** you up, your mum and dad.' Well, I think that's true. We all swear we'll do things differently when we have kids, and we do – but then there's bound to be something we do unknowingly that could help unhinge our children. And it's just being human and mortal and stuffing up.

Yes, my parents – in part – stuffed me up through absence, marital breakdown, and lots of other things. But I have to take responsibility, too. Ultimately we forgive those who hurt us, and pray that those we hurt might forgive us as well. I'm sincerely sorry that my mum can't be here to meet Jesse and that she's missed out on so much fun with my daughters as well. But I guess that's where the taking responsibility bit comes in. You get to pay the piper.

For me, the best parent in the world is my heavenly Father. He knows all about forgiveness and weakness – but also strength.

Strength and vulnerability – Jesus hanging on a wooden cross.

Fragile but never futile.

NICK'S NOTES

- ✔ LET GO OF THE PAST OR IT WILL HOLD YOU BACK.
- ✔ YOU CAN'T CHANGE IT – BUT YOU CAN CHANGE YOUR RESPONSE TO IT.
- ✔ FORGIVE THEM AND FORGIVE YOURSELF.

25

BIRTHDAYS

'A time to grieve and a time to dance.'
(Ecclesiastes 3:4)

They're landmarks. They're signposts. Birthdays can also be chiselled into our memories – particularly the key ones. For my eighteenth, I had a party at a disco called 'Samantha's' in Sheffield. Most of my year from school came. I loved it. We danced until our feet weren't just happy – they were delirious. I was young, and as far as I knew, immortal.

Well, at least it felt that way!

Three years later, I was on tour in Holland with the rock band Writz. Having spent the

I felt like I'd done a few **'life miles'**

night on the floor of a barge belonging to some Dutch Christians, I was woken by their singing choruses to me. I tell you something, if I'd had a gun at that point . . . However, worse was to come. Later that day, my band mates took it upon themselves to fling me unceremoniously into a picturesque canal in Amsterdam.

By the time I was 30 – and still resolutely single – I'd secured a steady job in the music business. And I was having dinner in our local Greek taverna. Much Retsina (a 2,000-year-old wine) was consumed. How come it never tastes the same back here in Blighty? It was a lovely evening with some dear friends.

Fast forward to 40 – and I was married with two kids. My mum had just died, and my wife was in the middle of a cancer journey that would ultimately rob us of one of life's great shining stars. The birthday party took place in our candlelit garden. I was on Prozac, a drug that helps fight depression. Mixed with alcohol, it also helps fight inhibitions. For someone who's fairly uninhibited anyway, this heady brew produced very interesting results.

Let's just say I didn't cover myself in glory . . .

> It's healthy to **reflect** on what you've **been through**

Finally, I hit the big 50 with two teenage daughters and a new wife. I felt like I'd done a few 'life miles'. We hired a local hall, filled it with all the people I love – and celebrated and thanked God. There were songs, speeches and a lot of frivolity.

It's wonderful to press the 'pause' button on your birthday. It's healthy to reflect on what you've been through, how far you've come, and where God has been – and hopefully still is – in the equation. It makes me think how Jesus viewed his birthdays. Just how aware was he of his destiny and what the future held? What would he have chosen to do differently – maybe ask God to select someone else; perhaps request time off on Friday?

And just where would we be if he hadn't taken the gravel road to crucifixion?

> **NICK'S NOTES**
>
> ✔ ENJOY LIFE – THIS IS NOT A REHEARSAL.
> ✔ CELEBRATE.
> ✔ INVEST IN RELATIONSHIPS.

26

THE ASCENT OF MAN

'We are trapped, devastated, and ruined.'
(Lamentations 3:47)

No, I'm not talking about the award-winning television series, but something much more basic. Yesterday I got up at 6.30 a.m. to take my daughter Jodie to school. I stumbled into the kitchen with one eye open to make my wife a cup of tea, pour myself a bowl of muesli and then let our canine chum Max out for a leak.

Max had an infection in his paw that had been treated and bandaged. But now, like a Houdini hound, somehow he'd managed to free himself overnight, chew at the wound – and make matters worse. So that was the first hurdle of the day.

Following family prayers, I de-iced the car and set off with Jodie for school – only to hear, after twenty yards, a loud grinding sound. We had a flat tyre. We limped back to the house, de-iced our other vehicle, leapt gazelle-like into it and sped off, trying to make up for lost time. Sadly, the steering was drifting to the left. Ever more conscious of the time and the need to get my daughter to her school bus, I quickly pulled into the local garage and checked the tyre pressure, which was down to just 10 pounds from 30 pounds. Suffice to say, I managed to get Jodie to her school bus on time and get home OK. And this was all before 9.30 a.m.

However, as I write, both cars are currently under the surgeon's knife at the garage in Chorleywood, having new tyres fitted and wheels balanced. When my colleague Gareth arrived later that morning, I happily regaled him with tales of my morning's woe. Safe in the knowledge that things could only get better, we drove off in his very safe and reliable Volvo. We were going into London to meet my old mate Marc Fox from the eighties band Haircut 100 – now a senior executive at the Universal Music Group.

On stepping into the lift, we were joined by a man who had the physical build and presence of the character Jaws from the James Bond movies. I'm not exaggerating when I say he filled the doorframe of the lift and his head touched the ceiling. Not surprisingly, the lift got stuck between floors. There were seven of us cramped together. I quickly divested myself of my cashmere overcoat (an expensive remnant from the nineties), and we pressed the alarm bell.

Jaws managed to prise open the doors

'Hello,' a voice said from far, far way. 'Where are you calling from?'

With ever-increasing incredulity we replied, *'A lift!'*

'What address?'

At this point I was beginning to panic. Our rescuers weren't even on site, but in a remote location. How charming, how quaint, how *very* inconvenient.

> I'd hate to be **trapped** anywhere for an **eternity** – other than heaven

Jaws managed to prise open the doors. We discovered we had no visible means of escape. Then the lift gave a small lurch. We heard noises that we all hoped were human help – not some automated machine still burbling at us from a distant command centre. Finally, after what seemed like an eternity but was probably only fifteen minutes, the doors, both internal and external, were opened and we stepped up and out.

I breathed clean air again. I felt my heart begin to return to its normal rhythm. And I couldn't help thinking to myself that I'd hate to be trapped anywhere for an eternity – other than heaven.

NICK'S NOTES

✔ TAKE THE STAIRS – IT'S BETTER FOR YOUR HEART AND MIND.

✔ IF TRAPPED ANYWHERE, TAKE A DEEP BREATH AND PRAY.

27

HOPE

*'Where then is my hope?
Can anyone find it?'*
(Job 17:15)

Hope springs eternal. Or does it? Are some of us more optimistic than others? As a rule, Christians cling to hope. The stuff of forgiveness and eternal life has got to brighten up the gloomiest of days. But what is it that makes us believe – sometimes against all odds – that such a thing exists? Is it because without it, the future would be way too grim to countenance?

I guess a starving child is ever hopeful of a full belly. A dying man is hopeful of a cure for his terminal illness. But are there circumstances where it's right to give up hope?

are there circumstances where it's right to give up hope?

Well, perhaps hope as we know it, yes. When it's obvious a person is dying, we may give up hope of their getting better in this life. However reluctantly, we may resign ourselves to their sad demise. I have done this three times in my life thus far. It never gets any easier – and neither does the pain diminish. If anything, it grows. But always there's this nagging feeling at the back of my mind. Not so much 'it'll be alright on the night', but more 'it'll be alright in the end'.

Maybe hope is delayed rather than denied.

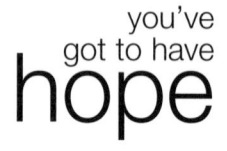

you've got to have hope

So no matter how dark and dismal the journey, I'm just not able to quit and give up on the idea altogether. For if there was no hope, there would be no heaven. And no heaven would mean no God and no Saviour – which would mean there would be no point.

That's right.

Nil points.

Not a sausage.

So you've got to have hope. Hope for the heartache, hope for the healing and hope for the hurting.

NICK'S NOTES

✔ EVEN WHEN EVERYTHING SEEMS IMPOSSIBLE, IT ISN'T.

✔ DON'T GIVE UP HOPE.

✔ DARE TO CARRY ON.

28

ONLY THE GOOD DIE YOUNG

'We ourselves are like fragile clay jars.'
(2 Corinthians 4:7)

I've just returned from yet another young man's funeral. Cut down in his prime by cancer, he left a beautiful wife and two lovely children. That family has been robbed of a husband and father. A few months back I was in the same church, to witness a tiny white coffin being brought in . . . so delicately. It contained the body of an eight-year-old boy who'd been ill for most of his short but bright shining star of a life.

> I do wonder why God hasn't **intervened** and taken out the **bad guys**

They say only the good die young. When I look at despotic figures like Mugabe in Zimbabwe, still staggering on well into his eighties, I do wonder why God hasn't intervened and taken out the bad guys. As time progresses I find I have more questions than answers about these issues, and they don't sit comfortably with me. My desire for justice is no longer satiated by a carefully worded glib textbook answer. It simply won't do.

Our faith needs to have integrity and to be authentic

Does it sound like a crisis of faith?

Well, it isn't. But as I look at it, I'm in a relationship with my Father God. So from time to time, just like in a marriage, the rubber will occasionally hit the road, and I think this is a good and healthy thing. Our faith needs to have integrity and to be authentic. I don't think we're called to listen to and repeat parrot fashion what the vicar says, without asking from time to time those difficult questions about the big stuff. You know – pain, suffering, life, death and so on. I also believe we won't find the answers to much of this until we get to heaven.

Poor old God. Can you imagine him, coming to greet people at the pearly gates – only to be hit with the same bunch of questions, over and over again?

If the fruits of the Spirit are love, gentleness, peace, patience and kindness, it's just as well he possesses those qualities in infinite measure. Otherwise we might receive our marching orders.

> **NICK'S NOTES**
>
> ✔ IT'S OK TO QUESTION THINGS – IN FACT, WE POSITIVELY SHOULD.
> ✔ DESIRE TRUTH AND INTEGRITY.
> ✔ TRUST GOD.

29

TREASURES OF DARKNESS

'The LORD is a shelter.'
(Psalm 9:9)

From time to time I get asked to speak at various events. That often leads to my talking about my life, and the highs and lows I've experienced. Quite often my audience will laugh and, by equal measure, cry. No, it's not because I sing to them (!) – though I could give Des O'Connor a run for his money. It's because something somewhere in my story touches them.

Sometimes life is just plain difficult

At the end of an event, they'll come and quietly share their own stories of heartache and loss, pain and sorrow. It's humbling – and a privilege – to hear them. I call these testimonies 'treasures of darkness'. These are stories about normal people who've often had to endure extraordinarily difficult circumstances. For a time they've been left completely broken. Like me, they wouldn't have chosen that experience. But somehow they've managed to make a good fist of it.

For the most part they've chosen to carry on believing, often in the face of apparently insurmountable odds. That they choose to do so is a testament to their faith and courage.

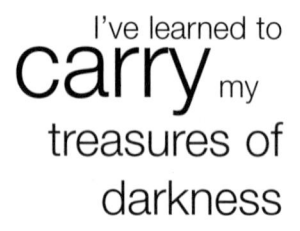

> I've learned to **carry** my treasures of darkness

Even some Bible heroes didn't do so well. Thomas doubted. Peter denied Jesus. I understand why they struggled. Sometimes life is just plain difficult. But it's in the struggling and wrestling with things that we get to grips with our faith. It's through such arduous times – even in our weakness – that we learn to become stronger. Like a tree that's grown from a sapling into a mighty oak, and withstood many storms, it may be a gnarly old thing blown this way and that. But it remains firmly rooted in the ground.

And that's where I find myself. I've learned to carry my treasures of darkness. They've helped shape me. Hopefully I've become stronger. They're like scars on a landscape that help to define and refine character. For when the wind howls and we feel we might break, often that's when God is at his finest.

We need to remain rooted in him and faithful to the end.

NICK'S NOTES

✔ MAKE SURE THAT THE 'TREE' GETS ALL THE NOURISHMENT IT NEEDS.

✔ STAND STRONG AND STAND TOGETHER.

✔ HOLD ON . . . ANOTHER DAY.

30

HAIR

'If a man loses his hair and his head becomes bald, he is still ceremonially clean.'
(Leviticus 13:40)

As a teenager, I was desperate for hair. Back then, I had no problem growing the stuff on my head. It was the 'bum fluff' on my upper lip and chin that bothered me. I was keen to cultivate the downy substance into something resembling – however faintly – a moustache and beard.

It took a long time coming.

Even now, if I let my visage sprout forth for a couple of days, I still have to join the dots with an indelible marker pen to resemble facial hairiness.

> **'bum fluff'** It was the on my **upper lip** and chin that **bothered me**

Initially, my chest was equally slow. For years in my twenties I had just three wispy strands. Now, as my hair so rudely scuttles off my head and what's left turns not so slowly grey, my chest could reasonably be mistaken for the thick shag-pile carpet in my son's nursery – minus the interesting stains. Another disconcerting development is my sudden ability to exponentially produce alarming tufts of hair from every available orifice.

> my chest could reasonably be mistaken for the thick shag-pile carpet in my son's nursery

So I have a veritable arsenal of appliances to deal with all this unwanted fur. Here's the inventory: tweezers (guaranteed to make your eyes water); nostril and ear trimmers for reaching the parts that normal grooming can't achieve; and last but not least, the device known colloquially as 'The Flaming Spaniard'. This is not to be tried on your own, but under strict supervision – and ideally with a sympathetic friend.

I first experienced this while under the influence in a barber's shop at Mijas on the Costa Del Sol. Our patron looked like a cross between D'Artagnan and Salvador Dali. After shearing my pate, with great and alarming dexterity he drew his cigarette lighter out of his pocket, shoved it in my ear, lit it, and just as smoothly replaced it from whence it came. He was like a gunslinger replacing his smoking gun in its holster after despatching the bad guys.

And here's the thing. I felt nothing. The experience was entirely pain free – and it worked. Obviously, if you don't like the smell of burnt hair, this is not for you. But as part of an afternoon's post-prandial entertainment, file it under 'Must see'.

NICK'S NOTES

✔ SHAVED ARMPITS ARE FOR GIRLS.

✔ KNOW THE DIFFERENCE BETWEEN A 'BRAZILIAN' AND A 'FLAMING SPANIARD'.

✔ NEVER LET ANYBODY NEAR YOU WITH HOT WAX IN THEIR HANDS!

31

THE BUGGY INCIDENT

'Why don't we hear the sound of chariot wheels?'
(Judges 5:28)

The other morning, while going about my many (ahem) fatherly duties, I embarked upon a wrestling match with my son's pushchair. I hadn't intended to get embroiled in such a violent fracas. But my position became untenable when I tried to collapse the thing so it would fit in the back of our Hyundai Tragic – sorry *Trajet*. It resolutely dug its heels into the ground and refused outright, without so much as a by your leave, to fold itself up. I was so incandescent with rage, you could have lit up the Blackpool illuminations – if you'd managed to find the right socket.

Why is everything so difficult these days?

We no longer have pushchairs or prams – now we have 'baby travelling systems'. The only possible reason for their existence is to fleece more money out of you and I by bamboozling us with lots of technical jargon and drawings. Your baby no longer has a blanket in his pram to keep his feet warm. Oh no! That would be way too simple. Now he or she has a 'cosy toes' available in a whole range of colours. How marvellous! How bloomin' expensive.

No doubt the umbrella – which comes as yet another hideously expensive accessory – is called a 'rain security system'. Yes, if only they could guarantee to keep the water out. That would be some rain defence you wouldn't want to mess with.

'Fetch my galoshes and hose, Delphinia – I'm going for a walk in the rain with our baby!'

'Oh Rory, you're so brave!' she coos while ovulating slowly, and wiping what is left of little baby Damian's breakfast off her heaving, ample, milky bosoms.

Finally, after much huffing and puffing, I managed to hoist the pushchair into the back of the van. Oh what joy unconfined! Happy in the knowledge that my little chore was done, I bounded into the house, only for my wife to pipe up:

> We no longer have pushchairs or **prams** – now we have 'baby travelling systems'

'Would you mind collapsing the travel cot as well? He might need to sleep while I'm at my sister's.'

I'd like to tell you the myriad of colourful responses that leapt into my head at this point. However, like a boxer bloodied but unbowed, I meekly threw the towel in.

'Yes, dear,' I said, dreaming of how one day I'd capture all the people who have ever designed these instruments of torture, put them all on some remote island and force them to watch endless repeats of *Teletubbies*. Then they might just understand what they're up against.

Eh-oh!

> **NICK'S NOTES**
>
> ✔ IF IT COMES WITH A MANUAL TELLING YOU HOW SIMPLE IT IS . . . AVOID AT ALL COSTS.

32

JOB TITLES

'If the master returns and finds that the servant has done a good job, there will be a reward.'
(Matthew 24:46)

In this politically correct age, where we're actively encouraged to affirm and nurture in our working environments, job titles matter. No longer do we pop into our local garage to talk to the car mechanic about getting our people carrier (by some minor miracle) through its MOT. Oh no. That's not how it's done. We have to book an appointment for our poorly vehicle with a fully qualified team of 'motor technicians'.

I think we should call people by what they do

A similar principle applies to the lovely ladies and gentlemen who help little children cross the road. From my dim memory of the 1960s (if you can remember them, you weren't there, etc.), they used to be armed with just a white coat and a sign on a stick bearing the legend, 'Stop'. We called them – quite rightly, I think – 'lollipop ladies' or 'lollipop men', and we viewed them as kindly, gentle folk. Now they retain the rather imperious title of 'school crossing wardens'. Which school have they upset? And why are they cross? Did somebody lick their lollipop when they weren't looking? I think we should be told.

> As a nation we've become daft about titles

A 'supervisor' in a shop – probably someone who is more qualified than you or me and may be nearing retirement – is now called a 'customer data administrator'. The hatchet man or woman of a large multinational corporation in charge of hiring and firing is called 'head of international human liaison'.

Trust me. You can't learn this stuff. It's a gift – given, I think, from birth – for all those born on the planet *Nerd*.

I think we should call people by what they do. A postman posts letters. Pure and simple. A teacher teaches. A gynaecologist ...well . . . Just why do people choose that as a profession? Curious, isn't it? I can't imagine spending my days looking at people's private parts, musing on their various shapes, sizes and afflictions – then rushing home to my wife to make love in front of the log fire. It might take the edge off it a bit.

So what's the point of all this drivel?

It is this. Words matter. We need to be honest about what it is we do and not try to dress it up to sound grander than it is. I write. So I'm a writer. Occasionally I write songs and then I become a songwriter. But I'd never call myself a composer. It's just way too pretentious. As a nation we've become daft about titles. We don't call a soldier a 'potential death technician'. He is a man employed by the Queen and her Government – often in extremely hazardous situations – who may be called upon to lay down his life in the service of his country.

Frankly, I think anyone in the armed forces, the police, the fire brigades, or the ambulance services should be described with just one word – 'brave'.

Now that's a job title I can work with.

And here's one last one – 'Saviour'. It was a completely exclusive one-off opportunity and there was only one man capable of doing it.

Jesus.

> **NICK'S NOTES**
>
> ✔ TAKE THE JOB GOD OFFERS YOU. BIG OR SMALL, IT DOESN'T MATTER.
>
> ✔ YOU MIGHT FAIL. GOD WON'T.

33

WHAT'S GOING ON?

'We are not fighting against flesh-and-blood enemies.'
(Ephesians 6:12)

This morning my daughter Jodie and I leapt out of our front door in a hurry, rather later than usual. I was anxious to make sure we got to Garston, in time for her to catch her school bus up the M1 to Harpenden. I wasn't in the best of moods. I'd really struggled to get out of bed at the requisite hour of 6.45 a.m. As our Toyota Picnic slowly lurched into life, we drove down the side of Chorleywood Common towards the M25.

> Even in Torywood, **feral youths** roam

Now, I really detest driving on motorways. At times I can allow for my less than perfect driving skills – but there's always some plonker willing to put his or her life at risk along with ours, by driving selfishly and far too fast. However, as we approached the motorway this morning, the traffic was more or less static. Then we saw the reason why. There was nothing on our side to slow us down – apart from the morbid curiosity of the silent majority rubber-necking at an accident as one poor individual fought for their life. The passers-by stared from their sanitized world into death's abyss and thanked God (if indeed they believed in him) that it wasn't them this time.

What's going on when another person's tragedy becomes so fascinating? What kind of society are we living in?

Last night my wife and I were walking home from a neighbour's Christmas party, with our son snuggled up in his pram. We witnessed a young man and two young women having a slanging match right outside our local church. They were clearly drunk.

You see, even in the middle-class ghetto that is Torywood, feral youths roam. Often fatherless, they lack discipline and a role model. Like everyone else, they're looking for love. They want to belong, which is why gang culture is so attractive to them. At least there, among their peers, they feel they have some sort of family – however fleeting that may be. They get mashed up, trash a few cars, shout and swear at anyone they like. Some will progress (*sic*) to relatively organized crime. Others will grow out of it and get a life. Some simply won't make it.

> we're living in a society where the 'man of lawlessness' is on the streets

What's going on?

Well, it's not rocket science or even rocket salad. I believe we're living in a society where the 'man of lawlessness' is on the streets. Laws and discipline seem to have been eroded over the past two decades – along with good old-fashioned family values. Loneliness has become an epidemic, not only among older society, but also the young.

You see, we all want to belong to someone, to have roots. And as Christians we need to model that not only in our families – but also in the wider community. No longer can we ignore the fact that weak government, lackadaisical standards, and a 'don't worry it'll be alright as long as somebody else sorts it out' mentality have failed our society.

Here's where the stuff hits the fan.

Don't leave it to the next person to come along and fix it. You do it. Let's have a return to real biblical living. It's alright if we fail. At least, please God, let's try. The Ten Commandments are a fantastic set of rules for us all. Even now, thousands of years later, they make such sound common sense.

What's going on? A fight between good and evil? Who will win?

Well, that depends on you and me and Jesus.

What are you going to do?

NICK'S NOTES

✔ TRY NOT TO SIT ON THE SIDELINES.
✔ PRAY FOR THOSE WHO ARE LOST.
✔ GRASP HOLD OF YOUR FAITH AND GO FOR IT.

34

GIVING

'Share your food . . . give shelter.'
(Isaiah 58:7)

It's so wonderful to give. Yet sometimes it's quite hard to receive, isn't it? How we give is important as well – to give freely and lightly – with no strings attached. We should take joy in the fact that it's a blessing to others, and a real privilege. To do it quietly, so the right hand doesn't see what the left is doing, is also good. Don't trumpet round the place what you're up to. It's not about looking good – it's about seeing the need.

Which reminds me . . . As I write, my wife would like to invite a complete stranger into our home on Christmas Day. Well, actually, it's an old friend from South Africa. Everything inside me says, 'No, it's our family Christmas, it's my son's first Christmas and it's supposed to be a special time.' Yet deep in my gut, something else resonates: *'I was hungry and you fed me, naked and you clothed me, homeless and you gave me shelter.'*

> It's not about **looking good** – it's about seeing the **need**

You cannot out-give God.

Bah! Humbug!

Don't you just love it when God has you bang to rights? Not! OK, I've just realized that if the lady in question does come, then I've already trumpeted it from the rooftops and you all know about it. Sorry, I'm just horribly imperfect and all too transparent. If she reads this at a later date, she is/was honestly very welcome. Sorry. I'm such a plonker.

Receiving is harder, though, isn't it? Sometimes it's because we're all too English about it, too easily embarrassed, too proud and too stuck up for our own good. And do you know what? I think it's time for us all to get over it! We've been given so much by God in this life, it makes wonderful sense to share whatever we can. Equally, when someone seeks to bless you, look upon it as a royal blessing from God.

Give freely. Give without hesitation. Give until it hurts.

You cannot out-give God.

He gave us his Son.

NICK'S NOTES

✔ BE MORE FLEXIBLE. GIVE MORE.

✔ LEARN HOW TO RECEIVE.

✔ PRACTISE BOTH.

35

THE LITTLE BOY AND THE SPARROW

'Dear children, let's not merely say that we love each other; let us show the truth by our actions.'
(1 John 3:18)

As a young child, I lived above the decorator's shop in Crumpsall, Manchester with my mum and dad and I had blind faith in all that my mum had to say. She was the fount of all food, love and kindness right? **'Why don't you go outside and try to put salt on a sparrow's tail?'**

However sometimes on Saturday afternoons, just before the wrestling with Kent Walton came on and her frayed nerves were about to snap she'd say, 'Why don't you go outside and try to put salt on a sparrow's tail? If you do, it will turn to stone.'

Now, fifty years on, with the benefit of near perfect hindsight, I can see she was clearly taking the proverbial, but at the time, as a child,

I believed her. How daft is that!

Which reminds me of another silly saying, 'I'll be there in two shakes of a donkey's tail.'

Think about it.

First you'd have to find your donkey. Second – and this is not for the fainthearted – you'd have to grab the tail firmly with one hand, while protecting vital parts of your body with the other and, finally, you've got to hope that the donkey in question is going to be in a good enough mood to let you get away with it.

This should never under any circumstances be tried with Spanish donkeys as they don't speak the lingo and they get a bit tetchy when they've had too much sun.

Back in the 70s Christians also would often appear to spout nonsense or ask daft questions.

'How are you with the Lord' was always a favourite of mine, and I was always tempted to reply, 'Bloody marvellous!', which could, of course, have given them the wrong impression . . . or maybe the right one. I mean, what an extraordinarily intimate question to pose.

But words can be funny can't they! When my father took me to Cole Bros in Sheffield to buy my first pair of long trousers for school, the shop assistant asked, 'Which way do you dress?' I very adroitly pointed out that it was on with the string pants and vest first, before tackling my socks. Everyone knew that! Of course he was, as I now know, referring to my willy and whether it favoured the port or starboard side. Once again, you could read an anomaly into even that apparently innocent statement.

So words are incredibly valuable and powerful.

'I love you' are three of the most amazing words on the planet, but do we over- or underuse them? Do we place more value in words or actions? If Jesus had said, 'I love you,' but had refused to walk the road to Calvary, where would we be?

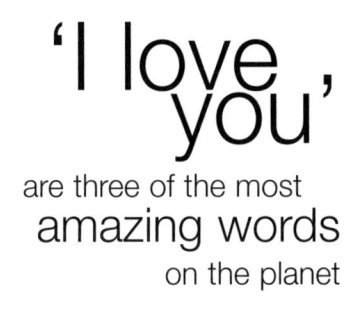

'I love you' are three of the most **amazing words** on the planet

So I think we need both – words and deeds.

And unlike the sparrow Jesus didn't choose to fly away. He hung around for ages.

> **NICK'S NOTES**
>
> ✔ SPEND YOUR WORDS WISELY.
> ✔ DON'T BELIEVE OLD WIVES TALES AND CERTAINLY NEVER PULL THEM.

36

CHRISTMAS

'Glory to God in highest heaven, and peace on earth to those with whom God is pleased.'
(Luke 2:14)

As I sit and type, Christmas is just six days away. Neighbours are popping in with cards, and our little lane is – for the most part – a joyful place to be. Not for us the sound of babies crying for food, or the foundations of a house shaking as bombs drop from an invisible and anonymous source. OK, so it says 'USAF', but they have no name and address to return to sender.

Meanwhile, the outgoing president of the United States is having to dodge shoes – not bombs. Lucky him.

for many years I **hated** Christmas

Back when I used to ride my funky moped with a guitar strapped to my back, I remember entering a competition with our little group Namesake to write and perform a Christmas carol. If memory serves me correctly, it was called, 'What Does Christmas

Mean to You?' Remarkably, we won, and I pottered off home on my wheels of steel very happy indeed.

But the truth is, for many years I hated Christmas. I found it a sad and lonely time. Frequently I'd traipse from one parent to the other, and the contrast could be quite stark. On one side of the park were arguments, cold and depression – and on the other comfort and warmth enjoyed by my father, his wife and my stepsisters.

The highlight used to be a bunch of mates getting together to have brunch and a few drinks at my friend Fiona's house, before hoofing it back for Christmas dinner and the Queen's Speech, followed by falling asleep and singeing my back on the gas fire.

Now, though, I rejoice that at last I feel *really* happy – and for the most part peaceful. It's been a long, long road, but I feel truly, wonderfully blessed.

And as I look into the eyes of my wife, and gaze at my daughters and newborn babe, I can marvel at the birth of the Christ-child and the love, sacrifice and restoration he still brings – centuries later.

Thank God for Christmas.

NICK'S NOTES

✔ DON'T BE AFRAID TO SHARE CHRISTMAS WITH A STRANGER.

37

DENTISTS

'Shatter the teeth of the wicked!'
(Psalm 3:7)

I've always had a profound pathological – and I think highly justified – fear of dentists.

My earliest memory of the 'White Coat of Terror' was in Manchester when my parents tried to take me to visit Phil McCavity – or whatever his *alter ego* was. I cannily waited 'til they'd got out of the car, and then locked all the doors. I was safe enough inside my dad's classic 1960s turquoise Renault Dauphine. Of course, I had to capitulate in the end as it was raining, and my parents were getting increasingly wet and angry.

It was also deeply regrettable that when I was young I had a small mouth and too many teeth, which meant I had to have four taken out. On the day in question, my mother forgot to give me the sedative to relax me prior to going under the

> When I was young I had a **small mouth** and too many **teeth**

gas. I arrived in a highly anxious state. Not only that – but one of the teeth he took out was the wrong one.

no one should ever take an appointment at tooth-hurty

So just as I was coming round, I had to go under again to have another taken out. That made a grand total of five. Suffice to say, when I next went to see him and he blithely told me I had a loose tooth, I leapt out of the chair faster than a speeding bullet leaves a gun. Later that night, after much jiggling, I extracted the offending molar in the bath at home – and realized the taste of blood is definitely an acquired one.

To add insult to injury, the dentist – let's call him Dennis Le Pain – rang my dad to complain (oh, the irony!), and I was forced to write and apologize to him.

As time has progressed, I've endured countless visits and put up with hygienists stabbing away at my gums with all the skill and dexterity of a professional darts player. Crowns have been fitted so firmly, I swear my jaw cracked in the process – as I spent the next four months in excruciating pain and whacked out on painkillers to cope with it.

Finally, though, I've found a dentist who manages to relax and calm me when I visit his palace of fun. It helps massively that he's a Christian and I trust him. It's never going to be a barrel of laughs, is it? And no one should ever, on any account, take an appointment at tooth-hurty. But love 'em or hate 'em, dentists are actually here to help.

If only we could swap places now and again. Now that would be fun, wouldn't it?

> **NICK'S NOTES**
>
> ✔ PRAY FOR PEACE BEFORE YOU GO.
>
> ✔ EAT AND DRINK MORE HEALTHILY TO COMBAT GUM DISEASE AND POOR DENTAL HEALTH.
>
> ✔ IF HE/SHE SAYS YOU'LL ONLY FEEL A LITTLE PRICK – RUN FOR THE HILLS!

38

THE SACRED LOAN

'My God is my rock, in whom I find protection.'
(2 Samuel 22:3)

Bit of a difficult one, this. But here goes . . .

A fair amount of my life has been pretty disastrous. Even though I'm inherently optimistic at heart, in a tiny corner of my brain I'm always expecting the worst to happen. Subconsciously, I'm preparing for it. I guess if I can look at the worst-case scenario and try to face it, then anything else is a plus.

> We all carry some sort of emotional scar tissue

For example, when my daughter goes on a Spanish exchange trip, at the very least I'm expecting her plane to crash and for me never to see her again. Similarly, when my wife goes into London to see her mates, she'll surely have an accident. Some moron driving mummy's 4x4 will shunt into the back of our Toyota Picnic, the car will be wrecked and she'll barely survive.

Horrible, isn't it?

This type of woeful, dismal, defeatist thinking is not what champions are made of – and frankly, it's no way to live (that's right, Battle, take yourself in hand). No, it's not right. But you *know* what I mean.

So having realized this, I've tried to set about retraining the way I think and also pray. In so doing, I've realized how deeply certain aspects of our character are engrained, and that they are often learned at very early stages in our lives. We all carry some sort of emotional scar tissue.

So what can we do?

Well, guess what? It's not easy. I'm slowly coming to grips with the fact that I have to have faith not only in God for my family's welfare – but also in them. I have to trust that they're smart and will know what to do. And try as I might, it's not up to me to spend every hour of the day trying to protect them.

It's simply not possible.

And there we have it. For us blokes in general, it goes against the grain to admit we can't fix something or look after somebody. But maybe they weren't ours to fix in the first place.

Maybe they're just on loan from a sacred person who never *ever* charges interest.

> **NICK'S NOTES**
>
> ✔ LET GO AND LET YOUR FAMILY FLY.
> ✔ LET GO AND LET GOD.
> ✔ LET GO OF THE PAST AND BEHOLD A BRIGHT NEW TOMORROW.

39

THE LABOURER

'Those who work deserve their pay.'
(Luke 10:7)

I don't know why it is, but for some reason, if you're working for God, people sometimes presume you can live on fresh air.

Let me give you an example. I received a phone call the other day saying that a group of people had been praying fervently and had decided that I was the right man to go and speak to them.

The journey to where they were would have necessitated a flight or boat trip and would also have taken me away from home for approximately thirty-six hours. I explained that I would need to charge a fee, as speaking engagements form part of my living, and that I would also need my travel expenses to be reimbursed.

> **if you're working for God, people sometimes presume you can live on fresh air**

There was silence at the end of the phone line, followed by, 'Oh. I see.'

I decided to grab the bull by the horns and said, 'I suspect you need to go and pray about that, don't you?'

> We simply do not pay 'the workers for the harvest' enough

They quickly hung up and I've never heard from them since. It was a rhetorical question.

Now imagine this. You work hard all week in a bank or a shop or whatever you do, and at the end of it your boss says, 'Thanks very much. You've done a great job. We really appreciate your efforts,' – and then he doesn't pay you a blinking thing!

How would you feel? Now don't get me wrong – I will, and sometimes do, go and speak for nothing, but I also use my spiritual antennae to sort the wheat from the chaff.

We simply do not pay 'the workers for the harvest' enough. 'Why?' I hear you ask. The answer is simple. We do not *give* enough. Think on this . . .

How much is your own salvation worth? What did God have to do to ensure it? What would you give to guarantee that all those you love would go to heaven?

Now look to your heart, and then in your wallet, and know this: *You can never outgive God*. Recession. Bah humbug!

God will always be God. Put your life and your wealth in his hands.

> **NICK'S NOTES**
>
> ✔ DON'T BE A SKINFLINT.
> ✔ DO PRAY ABOUT ALL YOUR FINANCES.
> ✔ GIVE EVERYTHING TO GOD.

40

THE SWEET SMELL OF SUCCESS

*'The L*ORD *has made my mission successful.'*
(Genesis 24:56)

Success is surely where preparation meets opportunity. Or is it? Is it true that nothing succeeds like success? I'm not sure.

> I think
> ## success
> is like a
> ## boxing match

Maybe nothing exceeds quite like it, and what is *it* anyway? How should we measure it? Is there one yardstick or loads of them? I think success is like a boxing match – but not necessarily one that follows the Queensberry rules:

'In the blue corner, the Heavyweight Champion of Greed, the Prince of

Darkness . . . and in the red, the World Super Heavyweight Champion of Love, the Prince of Peace!'

Cue bellowing, shouting and old ladies trying to get into the ring to club either party with their handbags.

It's all about choices, really.

I've got mates – some of them fabulously wealthy. They've opted to acquire all they can in material terms while eschewing the spiritual for now – or at least until they face their final curtain. Equally, there are lots of rich Christians who are more than aware of the extra responsibilities facing them. They step into the ring (quite often masked so as to remain anonymous) – where they may well receive a bloody nose.

> 'I'll labour night and day, to be a pilgrim

For me, though, the sweet smell of success is about my walk with God. Even as I write, I do know *honestly* how horribly pious that sounds. But when I'm close to him, that's really when I feel safe, secure, and truly unconditionally loved. Then as the old hymn-writer says, 'Fancies flee away, I'll care not what men say. I'll labour night and day, to be a pilgrim.'

And that's probably the best job offer we'll ever get.

Pilgrim.

Punching your weight
In love with life
Loving unconditionally
Generous with all you have
Relentless in your pursuit of truth
In love with your Creator
Men of character.

Yep, I'll have a go at that. Thanks very much!

> **NICK'S NOTES**
>
> ✔ DON'T BE AFRAID TO BLOODY THE OPPOSITION'S NOSE.
> ✔ ROLL WITH THE PUNCHES.
> ✔ REALIZE THE VICTORY IS ALREADY OURS.

THE GRAVEL ROAD TRUST

Was founded in 2009 by Nick and exists to engage with, equip and also empower people who are coping with loneliness and isolation as a result of bereavement.

Where appropriate, the Trust provides funding to meet the needs of families who find themselves in this situation.

For further information please contact:

The Gravel Road Trust
PO Box 375
Chorleywood
Herts
WD3 5ZZ
www. gravelroadtrust.info

Big Boys Don't Cry

NICK BATTLE

The Daily Male

NICK BATTLE

LOVE GOD, LOVE LIFE, LOVE LAUGHTER...

THE FINE ART OF FORGIVENESS

HIGH FIDELITY

THE BEAUTIFUL GAME
RECYCLING

THE CHUCKLE MUSCLE

THE HURTING PLACE.

MY BODY IS A TEMPLE

YOUTH IS WASTED ON THE YOUNG!

EAT YOUR GREENS!

WHERE DOES YOUR HEART RESIDE?

LUVVIES

RANTS, RAVES AND RIGHTEOUS INDIGNATION FROM THE AUTHOR OF *BIG BOYS DON'T CRY*

NICK BATTLE

In my dark despair   you found me,
wrapped your loving arms around me.
Deep down I know, you've
loved me from the start.
King of my
heart.

♥

KING OF MY HEART

Nick Battle Soaking In The Spirit

Let Go & Let God